MEMORIES OF
MIDDLESBROUGH

TRUE NORTH BOOKS
DEAN CLOUGH
HALIFAX
WEST YORKSHIRE
HX3 5AX
TEL 01422 344344

THE PUBLISHERS WOULD LIKE TO THANK THE
FOLLOWING COMPANIES FOR SUPPORTING THE
PRODUCTION OF THIS BOOK

MAIN SPONSOR
HENRY NEWBOULD LIMITED

ATHA & COMPANY SOLICITORS

REG BOYLE LIMITED

ICI CHEMICALS AND POLYMERS

THE CLEVELAND CENTRE

EVE GRAHAM LIMITED

GRECO BROTHERS

HILL STREET SHOPPING CENTRE

GEO HUMPHREYS & SONS LIMITED

G.W. LEADER LIMITED

RACE FOR FURNITURE

RELPH FUNERAL SERVICES

ST. MARY'S COLLEGE

UPTON & SOUTHERN PLC

First published in Great Britain by True North Books
Dean Clough
Halifax HX3 5AX
1998

ISBN 1 900 463 56 3

Introduction

Welcome to *Memories of Middlesbrough*, a look back at some of the places, events and people in the town which have shaped our lives over a period of around half a century. The following pages are brought to life by the selection of images from the not-too-distant past, chosen according to their ability to rekindle fond memories of days gone by and show how people used to shop, work and play in the town where they grew up. The chosen period is one which generally contains events within the memory of a large number of people in Middlesbrough - this is not a book about crinolines or bowler-hats! Neither is *Memories of Middlesbrough* a work of local history in the normal sense of the term. It has far more to do with entertainment than serious study, but we hope you will agree it is none the worse for that. It is hoped that the following pages will prompt readers' own memories of Middlesbrough from days gone by - and we are always delighted to hear from people who can add to the information contained in the captions so that we can enhance future reprints of the book. Many local companies and organisations have allowed us to study their archives and include their history - and fascinating reading it makes too. The present-day guardians of the companies concerned are proud of their products, the achievements of their people and the hard work of their forefathers whose efforts created these long established firms in the first place. We are pleased to play our part by making it possible for them to share their history with a wider audience. We have tried to create an interesting blend of photographs capable of informing and entertaining the reader. There are scores of images of local people in the book, deliberately chosen because many of them will have survived to the present time. We hope that these images will bring back happy memories for the people concerned and their families.

When we began compiling *Memories of Middlesbrough* several months ago we anticipated that the task would be a pleasurable one, but our expectations were greatly surpassed. The quality of the photographs we have been privileged to use has been superb, and the assistance we have received from the staff at the *Northern Echo* and

One of the great symbols of Middlesbrough, the Transporter Bridge, celebrating its 50th year of service in 1961

Middlesbrough's Reference Library combined to make our work very enjoyable. There is much talk in modern times about the regeneration of the local economy, the influx of new industries and the challenge of attracting new enterprise from other regions to Middlesbrough. And quite right too. We could, however, make the mistake of thinking that the changes are all happening *now,* but the reality is that there have always been major developments going on in the town. 'Change' is relentless and the photographs on the pages in the book serve to remind us of a mere a selection of them. Some of the images fall outside the qualification we describe as 'within living memory', but most of these will be familiar to us, either because they concern an event described to us by a close relative, or they feature monuments such as the unique bridges or buildings we simply felt compelled to mention. Whatever the view taken on the boundaries which separate 'history', 'nostalgia' and the present we should all invest a little time occasionally to reflect on the past and the people and events which made our town what it is today. *Memories of Middlesbrough* has been a pleasure to compile, we sincerely hope you enjoy reading it.

Happy memories!

Phil Holland

Phil Holland

TEXT: PHIL HOLLAND, PAULINE BELL
DESIGN: NICKY BRIGHTON, MANDY WALKER, MARK SMITH
LOCAL BUSINESS CONTENT: GARETH MARTIN

Contents

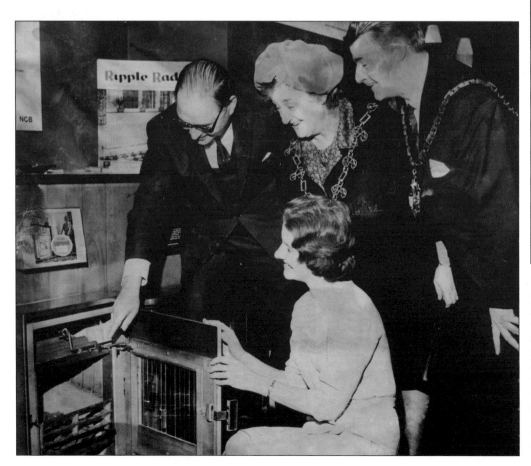

Left: The Middlesbrough Heating Centre showroom was opened in October 1964 by the National Coal Board and managed to attract over 4000 enquiries in its first few weeks of operation.

Events & occasions

Above: This lovely scene was one of many captured when the Prince of Wales visited Middlesbrough in July 1930. Middlesbrough was enduring difficult times when the Prince made his trip - and he was aware of it. He had a simple message for the town which was widely reported: "Your spirit will carry you through." In this picture local children, all members of either the Scouts, the Guides or the Boys Brigade, were assembled in the Boys Yard of the High School Grounds where they were to be addressed by the Prince. It was a long wait, and the excited children were entertained in various ways until the Prince arrived. In his speech he said: "Girls and Boys, I am very pleased to see you all here this morning. I have been told that you have been kept amused waiting for my arrival by a conjuror. I am afraid I cannot do you any conjuring tricks!" He went on "You will learn things useful to you in your organisations...play the game and good luck to you." Who could have guessed how things were to work out for the popular prince in later years?

Above: It was a wet day but the crowds turned out for this Middlesbrough Deanery Pageant despite the unpleasant conditions. The date when the scene was recorded is uncertain, but thought to be sometime in the 1950s. The leading lorry was one owned by local firm T.C Harrison, complete with religious tableau on the flat-back of the vehicle.

Below: This delightful photograph shows the re-opening of the re-laid Victoria Square in a ceremony which took place on 27th April 1949. The ceremony was obviously simple but dignified, and the main characters in the scene remind us of many old black and white British films which were so famous in the 1940s and 1950s. All the elements are in place to create a really nostalgic 'feel' in the picture - hence its inclusion here; the gas lamp, the broad white tape and the reporter, complete with notebook and raincoat in the background. Not to mention the policeman in his 'old-fashioned' uniform. Lovely! Wartime clothes rationing had ended only a couple of months before this photograph was taken; this was also the year that the Pound was devalued by a staggering 30% - indicating that in economic terms at least, Britain was not out of the woods yet.

Above: The Coronation decorations at the Town Hall and surrounding streets are clearly in evidence in this picture. It dates from May 1937 and relates, of course, to the Coronation of King George VI and Queen Elizabeth, later the Queen Mother. Four years later the King and Queen would thrill the people of Middlesbrough when they visited the area to inspect the wartime Civil Defence arrangements. As the Duke and Duchess of York the Royal Couple had visited the town in 1934 to open the Newport Bridge.

Right: Coronation Day in 1937 was a good enough excuse for a fancy dress competition - judged by the Mayor of Middlesbrough himself. Here 'Prince Charming' is seen being congratulated by the Mayor on his achievement while other children and the Lady Mayoress look on. The whole of Middlesbrough was decorated with flags, flowers and bunting as the town rejoiced at the Coronation of their new king. The people of Middlesbrough have always demonstrated strong affection for the royal family and this has been rewarded by more than the town's fair share of royal visits over the years.

Below: Prize giving was an extra-special occasion when these Middlesbrough children received their prizes from the Mayor and Mayoress of the town. Education in Middlesbrough began with the opening of the town's first school in Stockton Street in 1837. This establishment served to educate the 'infant poor' of the town and had a school roll of 120 boys and 100 girls. After the passing of the 1870 Education Act local School Boards were set up and Stockton Street School acquired the distinction of being the very first Board School in England.

*A joyful scene along Grange Street in May 1935. The celebrations were
held to mark the Silver Jubilee of King George V who had succeeded
Edward VII in 1910. The humble people of Grange Street had clearly pulled out
all the stops to the show the world just how much they cared for their King, even
the cobble stones were whitewashed in their display of loyalty and pride. The whole
town of Middlesbrough joined in the Silver Jubilee celebrations with street parties, a Civic
procession, and masses of elaborate street decorations throughout the town. A thanksgiving
service was held at the Cenotaph near Albert Park, attended by thousands of people. Sadly, George
V was to die within a year of the celebrations and the Country found itself in a constitutional crisis
over the love affair involving Edward VIII and the American divorcee Mrs. Simpson.*

Below: A charming scene from around 70 years ago. The occasion was the visit of the Prince of Wales to Middlesbrough, in the summer sunshine of 1930. The purpose of the visit was primarily to open the new Constantine College in the town. The police officers in this picture clearly had quite a job on their hands as they struggled to hold back the eager crowds - but it all looks good humoured enough. Reports from the day describe how 20,000 school children gathered to see the Prince of Wales at Ayresome Park. He was so moved by the spectacle that he suggested that the children should be granted an extra day's holiday from school. During the visit His Majesty laid a wreath at the Cenotaph in memory of the Middlesbrough servicemen who had lost their lives in the First World War.

Right: Shiny wellington boots and covered heads were the order of the day when this picture was taken in January 1949. Schoolchildren had been given the job of planting trees around Victoria Gardens in order to give the area something of a facelift. We know precious little about the occasion, save that it was clearly something of an honour for these two youngsters to be given such a prominent role in the tree-planting ceremony. We know too that the little girl in the picture was called Helen Fisher and we would be delighted to hear from her if this is possible. The years after the end of the Second World War were difficult for local people - as they were for most people in Britain. After the euphoria at the end of the conflict there were high hopes for increases in the standard of living for the general population but this was slow in becoming a reality. Coal mines, the railways, and the electricity companies were all nationalised, and, in 1948, the National Health Service was formed.

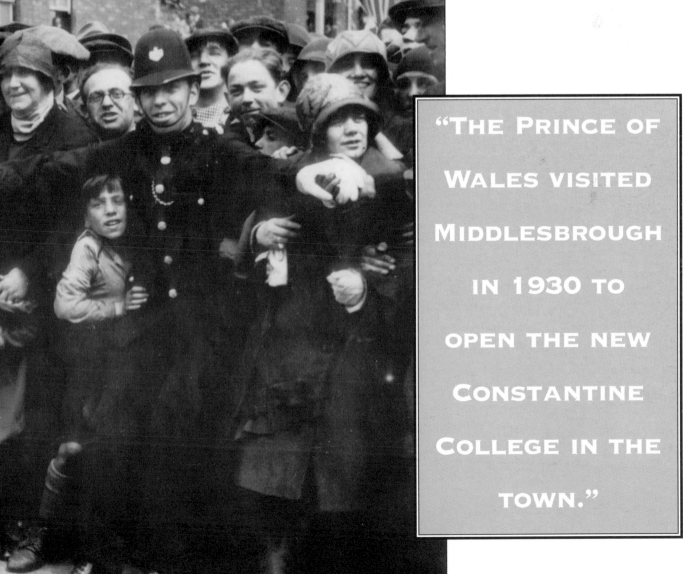

"THE PRINCE OF WALES VISITED MIDDLESBROUGH IN 1930 TO OPEN THE NEW CONSTANTINE COLLEGE IN THE TOWN."

The Battle of Britain commemorative service at the Cenotaph in Middlesbrough. The service took place on September 12th 1960. The town's cenotaph was unveiled on November 11th 1922. At the time this picture was taken the Second World War had been over for just 15 years, and thoughts of loved-ones lost in the conflict, and of the physical and personal damage that had been suffered during that time would have been fresh in the minds of those gathered here. The Battle of Britain had taken place relatively early in the war, in September 1940, just four months after the dramatic evacuation from Dunkirk. The townspeople of Middlesbrough had endured around 20 bombing raids during the World War II in which almost 80 people lost their lives. Virtually everyone was touched directly by the conflict - or knew people who had been. At least 8,000 properties had been damaged by the Nazi bombers and 300 of these buildings were completely destroyed. The Cenotaph, of course, stands at the entrance to Albert Park, a much-loved and well-used local facility which has served the town since 1868.

Left: This picture dates from August 19th 1941 and features Her Majesty Queen Elizabeth being assisted by Councillor Sir William Crosthwaite J.P the Mayor of Middlesbrough at the time as she alights from the entrance of a "Mobile Catering Canteen." The King and Queen had travelled to Middlesbrough as part of a tour of the North East boosting morale during the Second World War. This picture was taken in Albert Park. The royal couple were inspecting the Civil Defence Services in the area and here the Queen, later the Queen Mother, was inspecting the vehicle which was designed to provide emergency catering in the event of disruption to normal arrangements in the aftermath of a bombing raid. The mobile canteen was presented to the people of Middlesbrough by Lady Crosthwaite in June 1941.

Below: H.R.H the Queen, accompanied by H.R.H the Duke of Edinburgh visited Middlesbrough on June 4th 1956 as part of a tour of the North East. The young Queen was extremely popular at this time of course, the visit coming just three years after her Coronation. The crowds turned out in their thousands, lining the streets and cheering as the royal party passed. The Queen and the Duke of Edinburgh are seen outside the Town Hall, accompanied by the Mayor and Mayoress. At the time of the visit there was concern about the political situation in Suez, and within months a crisis would develop which resulted in an R.A.F bombing raid which threatened to take the country to the brink of another all-out war.

Above: Up the workers! Middlesbrough and the surrounding areas were not immune from the industrial unrest which which followed the return, by a landslide, of the Labour government in 1966. The government introduced a freeze on prices and wages which was not welcomed by many players in the trade union movement. It was also the start of long-running troubles in the British car industry. During the year 9000 workers were laid off in Birmingham when a strike by delivery drivers paralysed the plant. In this photograph members of the National Union of Seamen left their North Street Headquarters to march along Linthorpe Road en-route to a meeting at the town's Cenotaph at Albert Park. Their banners described their rather optimistic demands such as "cut the working week, but not our pay."

Top left and above: The Corpus Christi procession through the streets of Thornaby (smaller picture) and Middlesbrough (this picture) are featured in these two delightful early 1960s photographs. Boys and girls from St. Patrick's School, the Convent School girls, Pioneers, Womens' Confraternity Members and Young Christian Workers all took part (top left). The route covered over a quarter of a mile to St. Patrick's Junior School grounds and the pavements along the way were crowded with supporters. At the open-air service that followed about 1000 parishioners from St. Patrick's church sang hymns in adoration of the body of Christ. Note how tradition and a sense of respect for the occasion demanded 'covered heads' as the ladies in the picture make their way, with tremendous dignity, past the lead-covered bay-windows of this normally bustling street.

Left: Around 20 Fireman fought for hours to control this town centre blaze in 1971. Middlesbrough has had a fire service of sorts since 1855, but the duties were undertaken by the police at the time. By the turn of the century the fire brigade was being run on much more organised lines, with proper funding and a growing stock of officers, appliances and equipment with which to tackle the increasing number of fires in the town.

Below: The aftermath of a devastating fire which reduced Marton Hall to a scorched shell on June 4th 1960. One of Middlesbrough's most prominent sons, Henry Bolkcow (he was the first mayor of the town when it was incorporated in 1853, and later, in 1868, the town's first M.P) built the impressive building in the 1850s and entertained the 'great and the good' in the hall over a long number of years. An impressive collection of art was built up at the Hall during the time Bolkcow lived there. Henry Bolkcow began his working life on Tyneside in 1827. His success there allowed him to build up his fortune to the extent where he could embark on an ambitious project to begin iron making on Teesside. Marton Hall and its extensive grounds were bought by the well-known Middlesbrough Councillor Thomas Dormand Stewart, and handed over to the Corporation for the use of the people of Middlesbrough, opening as a Stewart Park in May 1928.

Tragedy on the Tees, in February 1966. Crowds can be seen looking on as a heavy tanker is hoisted out of the cold, murky water. The fibreglass cab had been crushed flat in the accident by the impact of the 50ft plunge to the river bed. The tanker had skidded on the slippery surface of the Newport Bridge, then crashed through the side of it into the river below. Sadly, the two men inside the cab died, despite the valiant efforts of rescuers who had battled for hours to free them from their upturned cab. The tanker had been carrying a load of sodium hypochlorite from the I.C.I Wilton plant to Domestos Ltd. as part of its regular daily run between Tyneside and Teesside. The accident led to an in-depth investigation by the authorities.

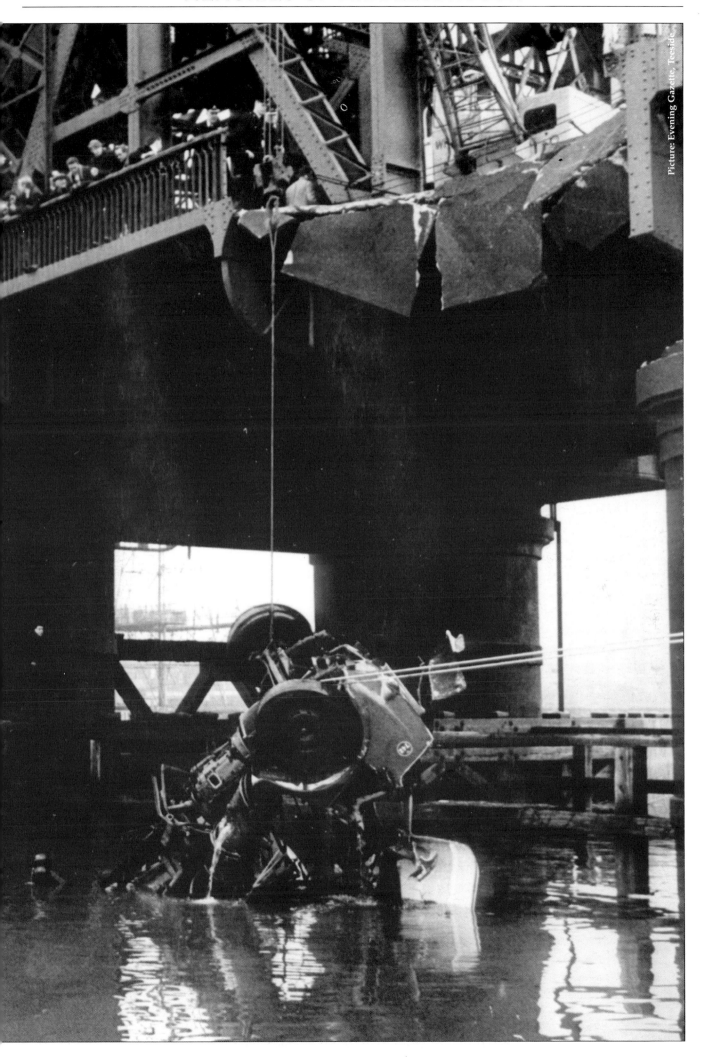

On the move

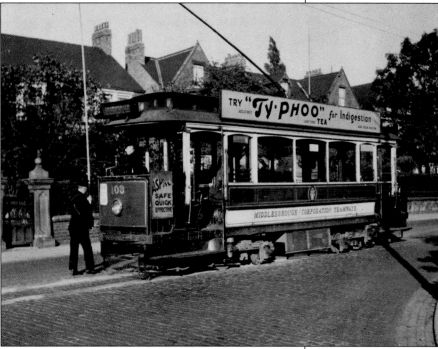

Above: "Ty-phoo for indigestion" was a bold claim made by the well-known tea makers which would not hold water (no pun intended!) today. The conductor working on this single-deck tram is seen manoeuvring his long wooden pole to relocate the trolley arm on the sturdy passenger vehicle, operated by Middlesbrough Corporation Tramways. But the picture was taken to record a much more significant moment in time than this otherwise routine task. The scene was set at the Linthorpe tram terminus (on the Linthorpe to 'Transporter' route) and the date was June 9th 1934. The significance of the photograph was the fact that this front-exit car was the last to run on Middlesbrough's tramways.

Right: The Transporter Bridge in Middlesbrough - perhaps the most famous landmark in the town, as it appeared in October 1961. The occasion was the celebrations for the 50th anniversary of the opening of the bridge and a party of civic officials is seen here, with the Mayor in the centre of the picture, being transported across the water in style. The first passengers to use the Transporter Bridge began doing so in 1911 after it was opened by H.R.H Prince Arthur of Connaught on October 17th. The massive construction had taken only slightly more than a year to complete. A terrific achievement by any standards.

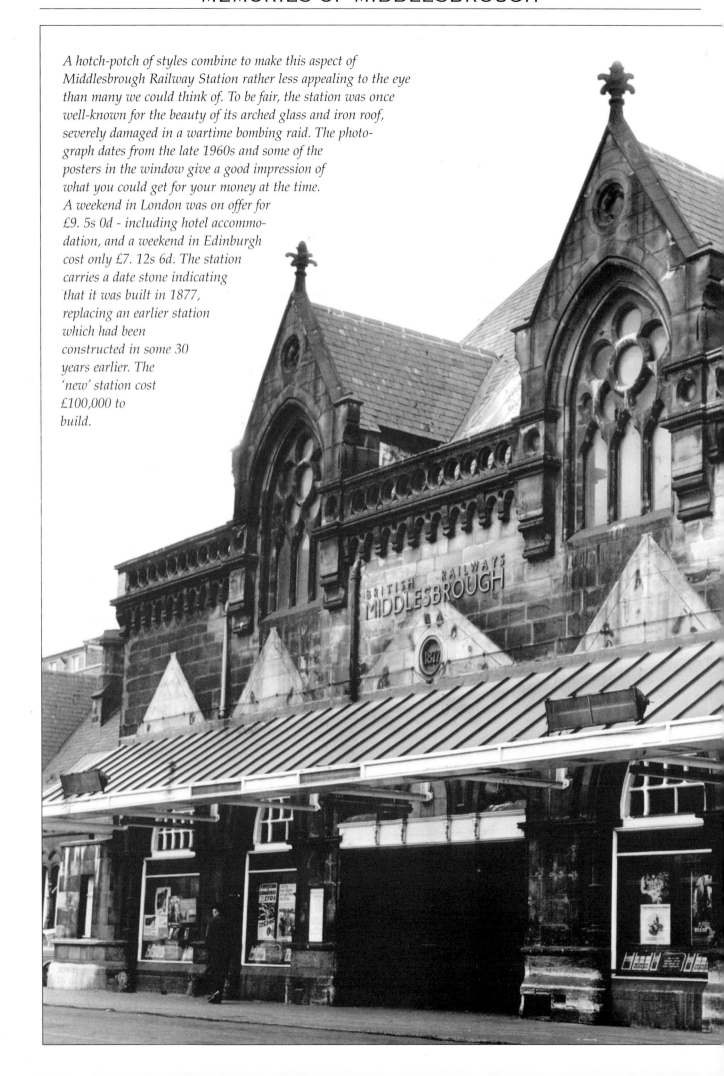

A hotch-potch of styles combine to make this aspect of Middlesbrough Railway Station rather less appealing to the eye than many we could think of. To be fair, the station was once well-known for the beauty of its arched glass and iron roof, severely damaged in a wartime bombing raid. The photograph dates from the late 1960s and some of the posters in the window give a good impression of what you could get for your money at the time. A weekend in London was on offer for £9. 5s 0d - including hotel accommodation, and a weekend in Edinburgh cost only £7. 12s 6d. The station carries a date stone indicating that it was built in 1877, replacing an earlier station which had been constructed in some 30 years earlier. The 'new' station cost £100,000 to build.

Above: The Newport roundabout was featured in this picture from 1968 to illustrate a story about road improvements. At this time it had been estimated by the local authority that traffic delays cost Teesside around £380,000 per year - though it is not clear how the boffins had arrived at this figure! The new £55,000 works had been approved by the Highways Committee and were intended to speed the flow of vehicles through the notorious bottlenecks at Newport roundabout and the Ayresome Street - Acklam Road intersection.

Top: This picture shows some of the area around The Middlesbrough Exchange and was taken in April 1965. The picture was probably taken to record the appearance of the new bus shelters. Note how they are free from graffiti - indeed, in the early 1960s, the term 'graffiti' was not even in common use. In the background the imposing building housing the headquarters of Dorman Long, the famous and highly successful steel company can be seen. Of course, that building has long since been pulled down, and the appearance of the whole of this area has been transformed in more recent times by the construction of the Albert Viaduct which serves to speed the flow of traffic along the A66 By-Pass.

The remarkable story behind Newboulds – Middlesbrough's oldest family business...

The origins of Middlesbrough's oldest privately owned company can be traced back to the middle of the last century. The award-winning family butchers and meat products business, Henry Newbould Ltd., is well known throughout the region and the story behind the birth and development of the firm is as interesting and dramatic as many a Hollywood screenplay or best-selling novel.

The story began with Wilson Newbould, the great grandfather of the present directors of the firm, back in 1856. At the age of 17 Wilson set out from his Dalton home to establish a butchers' business in Middlesbrough's increasingly busy meat market. This was a bold move for a lad in his late teens, but Wilson had worked out that the discovery of iron-ore would transform the small port into a thriving commercial centre of national importance with benefits for everyone involved in local trade. This confidence was well-founded, and as the population grew so did his sales of fresh, quality meat from his stall in the market. Early success enabled Wilson to purchase his first shop in 1862. His marriage to Jane in 1873 coincided with a move to larger premises at 10/12 Linthorpe Road. During this period Middlesbrough prospered. It was an age which saw the arrival of steel manufacturing and improvements in public health. Telephones and the supply of electricity became available for the first time and Wilson Newbould's business enjoyed a growing reputation which was soon reflected in his personal wealth and standing in the town.

Wilson's wife Jane was actively involved in the business working alongside her husband making the products for which the firm would become famous. At the age of 19 their eldest son, Samuel, joined the firm and early accounts describe him as being "a quiet lad, well-liked by all the customers." All seemed set for continued prosperity and happiness for the Newbould family, but this was not to be. Suddenly, and with the devastating speed characteristic of setbacks which would occur in the future, tragedy struck; Samuel developed pneumonia and died - a tremendous blow to the close-knit family and one from which Wilson would never recover. He died two days later aged just 57.

At the double funeral that followed at Middlesbrough's United Methodist Free Church, tribute was paid to the qualities of Wilson Newbould. He was described as "... a very distinguished man in public life, not that he was seen on public platforms or took part in great discussions, but he was one of those solid, quiet, steady-going men, whose very quietness covered a world of energy, and whose very manliness made it shown in his generosity and kindness. It does not matter with whom you talk, just know, all who speak of him respect him..."

It was 1896, the year before Queen Victoria's Diamond Jubilee. The burden of responsibility for the running of the Newbould family business was to fall upon Henry, the second son of Wilson and Jane. He was just sixteen years old at the time.

In Memory of

WILSON NEWBOULD,

Who died May 15th, 1896, aged 57 years,

AND OF

SAMUEL,

The Son of Wilson and Jane Newbould,

died May 13th, aged 19 years.

Top: Wilson Newbould, founder of the oldest family business in Middlesbrough. Above: The memorial service for the joint funeral of Wilson Newbould and his son Samuel and a page from Henry's diary for the week that Queen Victoria died.

Newbould worked hard alongside her son for the next nine years until her death in 1905. There followed the formation of a brief partnership with his younger brother Tom but this was ended after a short time by Tom's decision to seek a new life in South Africa.

During this time the practice of keeping a daily diary was established by Henry and these entries provide a fascinating insight into the development of the business along with the odd, and very revealing snippet of national news which adds to their interest for the modern reader.

A good example is the page for January 1901. The entry for January 21st reads "Pigs were dearer than ever at Thirsk"; more memorable was news on the following day, January 22nd "Queen Victoria died at 6.30 p.m aged 81 years 243 days." Henry's thoughts were firmly back to routine matters according to the following day's entry which read simply "Got new brawn tin."

Despite his tender age the business flourished under the guidance of Henry Newbould. What he lacked in experience he made up for with the boundless enthusiasm and energy of a young man determined to be successful in the world of enterprise. He took an abattoir in Brunswick Street in 1905 to process the pork he bought from the local markets.

He developed new products and improved the bakery behind the shop to the extent to which sales rose to £300 per week by 1914. His was one of the first businesses to introduce cash registers in Middlesbrough and the ever-increasing popularity of the shop is illustrated by the diary entry for

January 5th 1918. It read "Police had to queue customers."

His success continued after the end of the First World War and Henry moved to a larger abattoir off Snowdon Road to deal with the increased demand for pork. The pigs were delivered by train from the markets at Darlington, Thirsk and Newcastle. Henry and some of his staff would collect them at Middlesbrough station and herd them down the road to the abattoir. Occasionally, one would escape, to the amusement of passers by. One such escapee was eventually retrieved from a house on North Road much to the disappointment of the occupant who was looking forward to the prospect of plenty of pork and bacon for the coming weeks.

Henry had married Amy Bullough in 1905 and lived in Cornfield Road. Their first son, Harry, was born in 1908 and joined the company in 1925. Jim was born 7 years later and joined the company in 1935 after training with accountants, Chipchase Wood & Co. However, the sons were involved in the company as children and Jim remembers a sow bought from Thirsk was in pig and he prevailed on his father to keep the sow until the piglets were weaned. Henry agreed, but only on condition that Jim looked after the sow and cleaned out the sty every day.

This was a successful period for the business. Henry introduced the midget pies, known locally as 'Henriettas', which sold for 2 ½d for 2 and in 1931 he opened a second shop at Linthorpe Village in 'suburban' Middlesbrough. This was to prove an

Above: Henry and Amy on their wedding day in 1905.

In true British spirit other baking enterprises were quick to offer their help in order to get Newboulds' production back on stream again. This was wartime, and everyone was determined to minimise the effect of the enemy bombers and keep to a minimum the loss of valuable food production. Assistance came from other local bakeries operated by Hintons and Appletons, equipment stored elsewhere in case of such an eventuality was brought into service at the Linthorpe Village shop. Production, essential at this time of the country's greatest need, could not cease and due to the problems of space

an invaluable acquisition just eleven years later, when a German bomb landed on the original shop and bakery on Linthorpe Road.

Middlesbrough had taken a severe battering from the Nazi bombers and over 100 fires raged throughout the town at the peak of the raid. Newbould's shop was completely destroyed and a report from the time described how a fire officer and a colleague walked along the road in the aftermath of the attack. They were shocked, in the half-light when they stood on what they believed to be a naked corpse, around 100 yards from Newboulds. Their relief was considerable when they realised that it was, in fact, half a pig which had flown through the air from the pie shop propelled by the force of the blast! The night was the worst endured by Middlesbrough during the war. Sixteen people lost their lives and fifty more were injured. In all there were 75 other businesses destroyed in the raid, along with 68 domestic properties.

at the small 'village' shop, the sausage was produced in the yard behind, come wind, rain or, on one occasion, 6 inches of snow.

Running the business during the war brought many challenges for Henry and his son Harry. For one thing they had to manage without the help of Henry's other son, Jim Newbould, who had volunteered for military service. Additional difficulties were encountered routinely with the poor quality of the meat allocated to the firm and the call on staff for military service. Henry's letters to various ministries haranguing them about the quality of the meat, "it was green and sticky", and trying to persuade them to release a key employee from the call up, illustrate the pressures that modern managements do not have to consider.

Top left: The staff circa 1915 from left to right; Kate Hugill, Hagar Coverdale, Martha Griffiths, Flo Burns and Elizabeth Bell. Above: The note received by Henry Newbould thanking him for his early payment of Sur-tax. Right: The devastation wrought by Nazi bombers in 1942. Newboulds shop was completely destroyed.

There were other differences to the way business was conducted in wartime which are of interest today. The calculation of taxes was more reliant upon the integrity of business people, and their ability to negotiate a figure with the Taxman. Sur-tax was a form of taxation considered by some to be of an almost voluntary nature. A note from the Special Commissioners in 1941 gratefully acknowledged the receipt of £2756. 11s. 9d. which was paid to the cash-hungry government in advance of the due date. The note from their headquarters in a Llandudno Hotel is reproduced on these pages and gives an insight to the way business matters were conducted at the time.

Post-war expansion was the order of the day under Harry and Jim Newbould who had been demobbed in March 1946. The 'temporary' shop premises at 38

Linthorpe Road was purchased and re-fitted as a butchers - it had previously been a ladies dress shop - and a purpose-built factory on Longlands Road was opened in 1950 to satisfy increased demand from a growing number of stockists in the town and two new shops in Acklam and North Ormesby. Harry and Jim found time for outside interests too, each having played rugby football for Middlesbrough and Jim having a reputation as an outstanding golfer with many achievements under his belt, including the 1947 Middlesbrough Golf Championship. Everyone was sad to learn of Henry Newbould's death, at the age of 85, in 1965.

Henry had taken up the challenge of running the firm at an incredibly early age - and succeeded. He had enjoyed many of the good things in life and left a good foundation for his sons to develop.

Harry's son, Michael, joined the company in 1959, and helped at the increasingly busy factory. Newboulds wanted to remain at the forefront of developments which affected their industry, so Michael was dispatched to the U.S.A on a trade mission to assess the growing number of out-of-town shopping malls. Also among the party was

Ken Morrison, head of the Morrisons Supermarket empire. Their experience would influence the strategic direction taken by both companies in the years to come. For Newboulds it was the supply of products to the developing local supermarket groups like Hintons, and the acquisition of additional outlets in the new out-of-town shopping centres such as Billingham and Thornaby.

John Newbould, Jim's son, joined the company in 1971 after university, to help develop the retail and administration side of the business. Although computers are commonplace now, in those days they were not available to the average businessman who still used manual adding machines. John remembers his first purchase of a pocket calculator - it cost £50, a considerable sum at the time - and recalls his father Jim went "up the wall" at the sheer extravagance of the purchase and would insist on checking the accuracy of its calculations. The mid-seventies were the beginning of the technological age, but many of the old practices

continued. Sage was still grown at a farm near Thirsk, put into bunches which were hung to dry in the attic above 38 Linthorpe Road, before being prepared for use in the seasonings. The seasonings were still weighed by hand at the back of the shop by Jim, mixing was carried out by one of the assistants, or by John, who recalls, "Dad was weighing the pork seasoning and he was in a bit of a rush. There was pepper flying every where, poor Edie sneezed and her teeth flew out into the pepper barrel".

"A FIRE HAD STARTED IN A SCOTCH EGG FRYER AND SPREAD RAPIDLY THROUGH THE PLANT."

Jim's younger son, Peter, joined the company in 1978, as Harry Newbould achieved the distinction of becoming the longest-serving employee when he celebrated 50 years with the firm. The farewell party was held at the Dragonara Hotel (later to become the Holiday Inn) when friends and colleagues wished Harry every happiness in his impending retirement. An enjoyable night was had by all, but some would say that Harry had not quite grasped the concept of retirement when he turned up at the factory as usual on Monday morning.

The late seventies, now with nine shops, saw a drive to modernise the design and appearance of Newboulds retail outlets. The professional use of lighting and colour scheming techniques were first introduced at their new Hartlepool shop in 1979 to project Newboulds' image as The Family Butchers of the Future". The retail side of the firm was progressing well but there was potential, within sight but just beyond reach, to sell pies and other

meat products to the burgeoning number of supermarkets in the Northern region. To exploit this potential it would be necessary to build a new factory, with modern equipment and the capacity to produce high volumes of quality food products reliably. The property at Longlands Road had served the firm well, but it would be impossible to extend it and so the decision was taken to build a modern factory elsewhere. It was a major investment but one which was essential if Newboulds were to compete in this developing field.

The Riverside Business Park was chosen as a location and the new factory was completed in 1985. Much thought went into ensuring that the factory was capable of efficiently supplying a wide range of pies, savoury products, cooked meats and sausages to the retail and catering sectors. The investment paid off and sales grew rapidly. It was another time in the history of Newboulds where everything seemed to be in place for a period of stability and expansion. This was not to be, and a telephone call to John Newbould before dawn on November 27th 1986 was to threaten the livelihood of every member of staff at the firm as well as the very existence of the company, despite its 130 year pedigree. When John Newbould took the 'phone

Right: *The dreadful sight of the remains of the new factory following the devastating fire in November 1986.*
Opposite page: *Two views of Newboulds shop in the 1950s.*

which had been so difficult to win over the previous two years, were all lost.

The factory was re-built to even higher standards with the latest in modern machinery. Newboulds returned to the Riverside Park site just less than a year after the fire, in October 1987 and set out a five-year mission to rebuild their customer base. John re-built their wholesale business and helped Peter increase their shops to a total of 15, while Michael organised the factory which now supplies many high street retailers with the award winning meat products for which it has become known throughout the country.

Newboulds remains a family business; Managing Director John Newbould is in no doubt that this close relationship with the community is the main reason for the company's survival. He recalls attending a party to celebrate the 50th Anniversary of Heagney's Supermarkets; he was presented with an old 2lb weight stamped 1942 which was from the bombed out shop on Linthorpe Road. It had been returned by two ladies who had rescued it from the rubble and kept it as a memento; both now in their 80s, they wished to return it to Mr Newbould. This special relationship with the community was recognised at the Teesside Business Awards in 1996 presented by Rt Hon John Major, MP, when the company won the award for

call his first reaction was to ask "Is it insured?", thinking that the caller was referring to the old premises which were still unsold. His heart sank as the voice at the other end of the line said coldly "John, it's the new factory." On arriving at the site the management team found the twisted remains of the business they had put their heart and soul into. A fire had started in a scotch egg fryer and spread rapidly through the plant. It would take a super-human effort to keep the business going over the coming months.

The work began immediately. Local companies, particularly Morgans and Amberley Foods helped with machinery and temporary premises because the old factory along Longlands Road had been vandalised during the time it had been unoccupied. The 'wartime spirit' that had saved the company some 44 years earlier, returned to save the day again. The staff worked long hours in difficult conditions, some went to produce sausage in Sunderland at night, others travelled to Whitby to cut up pork in the early hours of the morning or produce pies at Morgans Bakery after normal working hours. The magnificent efforts of all the staff and the help received from many local companies went far beyond the call of duty. As a consequence the business survived, but the valuable orders and contracts

Top: The award winning Newbould's shop on Linthorpe Road. Above: Triumphant staff outside the shop, celebrating their award as the "Best Butcher in Britain".

'Business in the Community'.

Louise Newbould, Michael's daughter, is the latest family member to become involved with the firm. After joining the company from Edinburgh University in 1990 she went on to manage activity in the crucial areas of quality control and product development. The challenges now facing Newboulds and other food producers were not bombs or fires, but food safety scares. John remembers how, at the start of the BSE scare, he flew to the Orkney Islands to secure supply of a particular sort of beef. The flight alone cost £405 - a return flight to the USA would have been cheaper at the time. It was a hectic day out from the office, visits to farmers and the abattoir, as well as radio and TV news interested why this Englishman from the 'Sooth' was in Orkney. The day was complete when John found that the pork pies sold at the Presto supermarket in Kirkwall were made by the firm. He bought two as proof of his find. The weather was appalling for the return flight. The flimsy propeller driven aircraft was to be flown by a casually dressed man who claimed he normally worked in the office. He added that the luggage and the catering was being taken off the plane because of the adverse conditions, but the passengers could remain. A nervous John was sustained by his pies, but the evidence of his find was lost.

throughout the UK. Newboulds achieved a record 95% score in the contest which was judged on the quality of the meat offered, hygiene standards, customer service and community care. The trophy and £2000 cheque was awarded in a grand ceremony at the Dorchester Hotel in London and it was entirely typical of Newboulds that the money was shared out amongst the staff in recognition of their contribution to the company's proud achievement.

The company continues to grow through supply to external organisations and acquisition of new retail outlets which now total 22 after the take-over of the Munro chain of butchers shops. In terms of its location the business has come full-circle, as its Head Office and factory is located just a short distance from St. Hilda's where the story of Newboulds began. Despite the tremendous challenges over the years which would have spelled closure for many less determined firms, Newboulds has come through with flying colours and is in great shape to cope with the increasing demands being made on companies involved with the food industry.

Newboulds are now building partnerships with local suppliers to produce beef, pork and lamb to their requirements and standards, although John points out that he does not set the standards, his customers do. Recognition of the high standards achieved by Newboulds have come in a variety of forms. 'National Display Winner', 'Pork Product of the Year', 'Enterprise Award Winner', and in 1996 they were named 'Best Butcher in the North'. Then in 1997 the firm was judged the 'Best Butcher in Britain' by the Meat Trades Journal, beating off stiff competition from hundreds of other butchers

In the 1850s Wilson Newbould said, with amazing foresight, that "Quality is the order of the day." This remains the philosophy of the company, supported by a respect for the needs of every individual customer which sets *Newboulds* apart from their rivals in the meat trade and protects their position as the oldest and largest butchers in Teesside. Wilson Newbould really would have been proud!

*Top: Members of the Newbould family celebrate the opening of the new factory in 1985. **Above left:** The rebuilt state-of-the-art factory near St. Hilda's in 1987.*

At your leisure

*This very thought-provoking picture shows
the Mayoress Mrs Kedward, visiting her old school
in 1929. It is clear from the picture that the children
shown here didn't have much, these were difficult times for
people in Middlesbrough, as elsewhere in Britain, but the
Christmas tree looks full of toy aeroplanes, games, dolls and toy toolkits
which would have kept the children excited for many days before the big day
arrived. As usual, in a scene of this nature, the footwear worn by the characters
tells a story. The variety of wellington boots, clogs and sandals will bring back
memories among our most senior readers, there was obviously precious little cash around to
spend on childrens' clothing. Note the little girl on the left of the picture, holding her ears as the
photograph is taken. We wonder if this was the second attempt at a picture taken with the aid of 'flash
powder' which would have made quite a bang as well as creating the necessary light for the picture. If this
were so then the girl concerned would have been anticipating the unwelcome sound by covering her ears!*

"THERE IS SOMETHING ALMOST ARTISTIC ABOUT THE WAY THE TRICYCLE CONTRASTS WITH THE GRIMY HOUSES AND THE HUGE INTIMIDATING GAS HOLDER."

An extraordinary scene from 1963, dominated by the huge gas holder in the distance which dwarfs the street of terraced houses and the children playing outside them. There is something almost artistic in the way that the shiny new tricycle in the centre of the scene contrasts with the modest grimy houses and the huge, intimidating gas holder behind them. The little lad would have been the envy of all his friends with his blue and yellow *Sunbeam Winky* tricycle complete with 'luggage boot' and pneumatic tyres. I know I was! Cannon Street itself was the scene of two historic street disturbances which hit the headlines throughout the country. In 1926 mounted police were stationed nearby as tension rose in the General Strike. Then in August 1961 the community was torn apart once more in street violence which flared up in the neighbourhood, resulting in a show of strength by the police to regain order.

Above: A delightfully tranquil scene captured at Ayresome Gardens in 1966. The immaculate flower beds and well-kept lawns were a credit to the gardening staff, and the semi-circular arrangement in the foreground, complete with carefully laid-out 'football pitch' were included to celebrate England's victory in the World Cup competition. The floral writing around the perimeter of the display reads "World Championship Jules Rimet Cup England" and "Middlesbrough 1966."

Top: With some irony, this photograph was taken to record the appearance of the newly-completed Park Road North diversion. It dates from October 1954. On the left the Cenotaph is visible, the focal point of many of Middlesbrough's most emotional public occasions, now provided with the ideal surroundings for times such as those. To the right of that evocative monument is the Dorman Memorial Museum which was opened in July 1904 as a memorial to the town's menfolk who lost their lives in the South African Boer War. It was a gift to the town from Sir Arthur Dorman, the wealthy industrialist, who lost a son in that conflict.

Children can be seen enjoying the fine weather in Albert Park in May 1936. It is a sobering thought to reflect on how most of those featured here will be in their seventies at the time of writing. How innocent they were then. Their lives would be changed forever by the war years which followed before they became much older. Times were hard in the mid 1930s as evidenced by Jarrow's unemployed workers and their trek to London. Albert Park was given to the people of Middlesbrough in 1868 by the great benefactor Henry Bolkcow. The park was opened by Prince Arthur in 1868 and named after his father Prince Albert. During 1936 a crisis of succession affected the monarchy in Britain. After the death of George V, Edward VIII was due to succeed him. Instead, the new King decided to forego his right of accession and marry instead the American divorcee Wallace Simpson. After the biggest crisis to hit the monarchy for centuries the Duke of York became King George VI.

Above: The Showboat Night Club was situated in Wilson Street, Middlesbrough. A nautical send-off was ensured in 1968 by the presence of the Mayor of Teesside Alderman Jack Brown who was piped 'aboard' by local members of the Sea Cadets. More than 1,000 guests attended the champagne send-off for the lavish club which had had £150,000 spent on it in it s conversion from a dance hall. Here we see an interesting spelling of the word 'Middlesbrough! '
Other show business news from 1968 included the tragic suicide of Tony Hancock (1924 - 1968) in a hotel room in Sydney, Australia. He had become a popular household name with his radio show "Hancock's Half Hour."

Right: The corner of Linthorpe Road and Southfield Road, and the Gaumont Cinema featured in this picture as news spread that the site had been acquired for redevelopment. The building started life as The Grand Opera House in December 1903. After just-short of 30 years the establishment became known as the Gaumont Cinema, bowing to the increasing popularity of film-going which was boosted by the introduction of the 'Talkies.' Incidentally, the first 'talking picture' to be shown in Middlesbrough was 'The Singing Fool', starring Al Jolson, in 1929. By the 1960s the popularity of cinema-going had gone full-circle as the age of television and bingo took over. The writing was on the wall for the Gaumont and there was more than a hint of sadness when it closed its doors forever on February 29th 1964. The site was later cleared and re-developed.

Below: In the summer of 1969 the mothers of Holt Street were so determined to create a safe place for their children to play that they threatened to barricade the street to form a playground. Success for them was achieved when the *United Bus Company* came to the rescue with an offer to let them use this piece of spare land behind one of the bus station - at least until the end of the school holidays. As an aside, it is interesting to remember one of the events which was shaping the world at the time these ladies were fighting their battle with the local authorities. Neil Armstrong had the honour of being the first man to walk on the moon at the zenith of the Apollo programme on 21 July 1969.

"THIS WAS THE AGE OF 'FORMICA' AND PVC UPHOLSTERY."

Above: It is not known precisely when the age of 'fast food' officially arrived in Middlesbrough, but a milestone was certainly passed when the 'Gingham Kitchen' opened in 1966. It was located at 176 Linthorpe Road. To the modern eye this scene could be taken from a set from "Thunderbirds", such is the design of the 'futuristic'- now nostalgic - furniture.

This was the age of formica and PVC upholstery, of bold stainless steel lampshades and varnished pine ceilings.

The caption on the rear of the print informs us that the picture on the wall was one of Barry Leighton-Jones' original prints. Some of the customers look a little uncertain in their modern surroundings, but the gent in the far corner looks entirely at home in his warm car-coat (another icon of the times) tucking into his full English breakfast.

Perhaps he was a thrusting sales executive, with Hillman Minx parked outside (few parking restrictions in those days) and pocketful of luncheon vouchers ready to take on the world of commerce? 'Eating out' in the mid 1960s was nowhere near as common-place as it is these days. Restaurants in the major stores - catering mainly for shoppers and lunchtime meals for office workers did a good trade, but other than the very occasional Chinese and Indian restaurant, there were relatively few places catering for sit-down meals. Coffee bars with the Juke Boxes and loud frothy-coffee machines were popular in the 1950s and 60s, but we had to wait a few more decades for the era of 'fast-food' to really take hold.

Above: An open-air exhibition of paintings took place in Victoria Square, recorded by this photograph in 1957. The officials seen in the picture include Mrs. Ethel Guymen, Lady Dugdale, F.J. Longstaff and Mr. John Slater. This was the year that Britain exploded her first hydrogen bomb and drew the first Premium Bond prizes in the newly created scheme to promote public savings. In the Arts, critical acclaim was achieved on the release of David Lean's film "The Bridge on the River Kwai."

Right: This demonstration of a solid fuel heating appliance was given by Miss Mavis Robinson of Darlington in the 'new' Middlesbrough Heating Centre. The showroom was opened in October 1964 by the National Coal Board and managed to attract over 4000 enquiries in its first few weeks of operation. During the opening ceremony the regional chairman of the N.C.B described the benefits of solid fuel heating and added that new customers would also be helping to keep British miners employed. The Mayor of Middlesbrough, Coun. A. H. Barrass said the importance of the centre was obvious in view of the increasing number of smokeless zones being introduced and the need to find more advanced types of solid fuel. Pictured here are Dr. W. Reid of the NCB, the Mayor of Stockton, Councillor Mrs. M. Scott and the Mayor of Middlesbrough, Councillor E. H. Barrass, along with Miss Robinson.

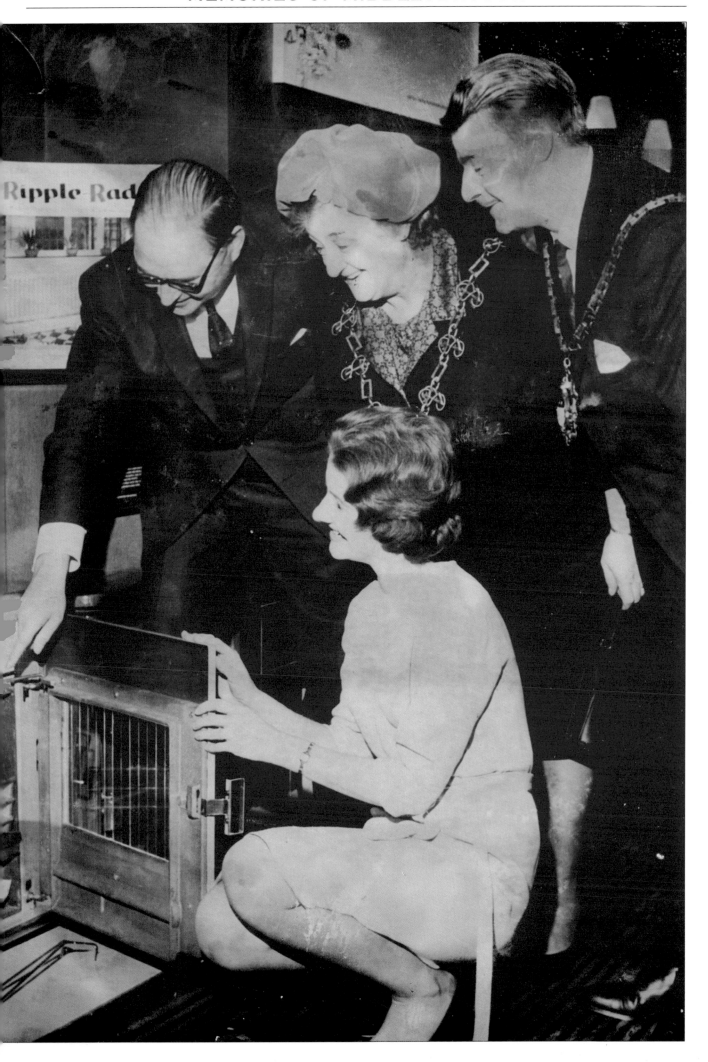

Sporting life

Right: The Middlesbrough Football ground as it appeared in 1934. Major improvements had been made to the fabric of the ground around five years earlier with the introduction of concrete terracing. The signs on the covered stands were an early form of ground advertising and paid for by two firms - "Stantonia Footwear" and "Taylor's Coal." Interestingly the major proportion of the accommodation at the ground was for 'standing' spectators. Not surprising considering the massive crowds which could be attracted to matches and the need to cram them into the ground. Note too, that despite the number of roads and houses there are in the picture it is difficult to spot any evidence of motor transport whatsoever.

Below: All eyes were on the Athletics track at the Clairville. This meeting took place in 1963. Sport and recreation have always been very popular in Middlesbrough. Middlesbrough Football Club was founded in 1876 and played its first match in 1877 on the archery area of Albert Park. Middlesbrough's Cricket Club was established rather earlier than the football club, at a ground on Albert Road in 1855. The better-known Acklam Park ground, on Green Lane, was opened in 1933.

Bottom: Middlesbrough, indeed the whole of the country was gripped by football fever when this picture was taken, for it was March 1966, the eve of the World Cup competition which would ultimately be won by England. This picture shows Middlesbrough's first team squad consisting of: **Back Row:** (left to right) Stan Anderson (Coach) Jim Irvine, Bill Gates, Alec Smith, Des Mc Partland, Neville Chapman, Bryan Orritt, Ian Davidson, George Wright (Physio and Trainer). **Front Row:** (left to right) Dickie Rooks, Eric Mc Mordie, Billy Hornes, Derek Downing, Jim Townshend, Bobby Braithwaite, Gordon Jones.

Below: Three members of the North Korean Football Association delegation visited Ayresome Park to inspect the ground and pitch that would be used for some of the preliminary matches in the 1966 World Cup Competition. Three matches were played here as part of the World Cup Competition. The delegates can be seen here with the popular Middlesbrough back-room operator, Secretary Harry Green, as he gives the delegates the 'inside track' on the ground and its facilities. Ayresome Park was not the first ground to be used by Middlesbrough F.C. The first matches were played at the Old Archery Ground in Albert Park. The highest gate recorded at Ayresome Park was 53, 802 in December 1949.

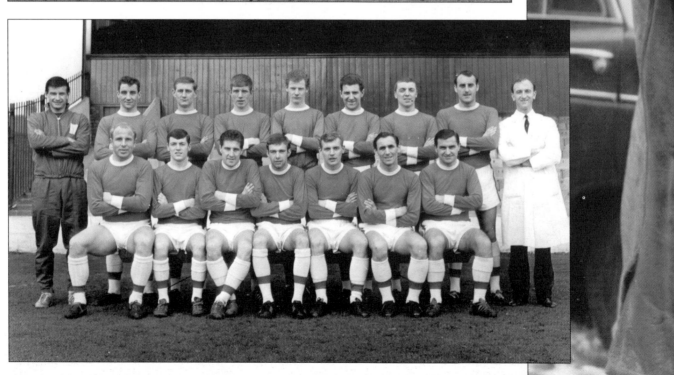

Raich Carter with the obligatory sheepskin three quarter-length coat, outside the Middlesbrough ground at Ayresome Park. It was a sad time for him, as he had just been relieved of his duties as team manager by Club Chairman J. Eric Thomas. The post was filled in the interim by Harold Shepherdson the former assistant manager and England trainer. Concern had been rising at the mediocre position Middlesbrough held as the end of the season approached. There were, in fact, 16 matches left to play, including 10 away games. Raich Carter had had a distinguished career in football; the inside-right for Sunderland and England had also managed Hull, Leeds and Mansfield.

Around the town centre

An unusual picture of Middlesbrough Railway Station dating from April 1954. Keen eyes may just be able to make out the tiny figures of the brave men on top of the iron-work which had been badly damaged in the notorious wartime bombing raid of July 1942. The glazed roof was about 900 feet long and must have been an awe-inspiring sight for the townsfolk of Middlesbrough to behold when it opened in 1877.

Left: An interesting view of the old Post Office building, seen on the left of the picture and destined to become the location of the Cleveland Archive Service. On the right of the view is Jordison's Printers, a company steeped in history and once described as the finest quality printers in the country. Next to Jordison's the Masonic Hall, with its distinctive round window above the door, is just in view. All the property described here, with the exception of the old Post Office building, has now been cleared. In the foreground, safety railings which formed the perimeter of the old Exchange Bus Station can be seen. Again, these disappeared when the Albert Viaduct was constructed to carry traffic on the busy A66 northern route.

Top left: A scene which manages to capture the spirit of ordinary daily life in Middlesbrough. It was recorded at the junction of Newport Road and Corporation Road and is thought to date from around 1930. *Binns*, the department store which has been a part of the lives of so many local people can be seen on the right of the picture. The first Binns store in Middlesbrough was opened in 1923 in a store formerly owned and operated by Thomas Jones at the junction of Linthorpe Road and Newport Road. Binns were later taken over by the House of Fraser group of department stores.

Left: The Royal Exchange situated at the corner of Wilson Street is featured here in a photograph from September 1938. The boards outside the building advertise luncheons and teas at 'moderate prices', though it unlikely that many of the men seen on the corner of the street would have been able to afford them. The Royal Exchange Buildings date from 1868, though they replaced an earlier facility which was first opened in 1838. Sadly the fine old building was pulled down in the mid-1980s to make way for a new road system. When it was built it cost the considerable sum of £28,000 - more than had been anticipated at the time, and the construction of a grand tower which had been part of the original design had to be abandoned due to the lack of funds. The Exchange was the place that people trading in iron, steel and other locally-produced commodities would meet (on Tuesdays and Fridays) in order to negotiate the price of these goods, all of which were crucial to the local economy.

Below: A view along an almost deserted Linthorpe Road which dates from the 1960s. In the distance is an Austin 1100 - these vehicles were introduced in the early 1960s and were way ahead of their time in terms of interior spaciousness, ride quality and economy. Sadly they were prone to serious rust in later life and few of them survive. Several well-known company names can be seen in this picture which are bound to bring back memories, including Maynards, Halfords and the ABC cinema. On the left of the street, as we look at it, is TeleHire, with a promotion in the window enticing new customers with the offer of 3/- (15p) off in the pound.

Right: Bottomley Street as it appeared in the early 1960s is featured in this photograph from the time. The MacFisheries shop can be seen on the right of the picture - it was always very popular with local people in the area. Character is given to the scene by the selection of 1960s motorcars in the picture and the open cart used as a mobile fruit and vegetable stall.

Above: Victoria Square and the Municipal Buildings, overlooked by the graceful clock tower of the Town Hall are seen in this picture from the 1950s. The Central Library building is shown on the right of the picture, it was opened in May 1912, thanks to a £15,000 contribution by Andrew Carnegie the well-known philanthropist, and thanks also to the donation of a piece of land by Sir Hugh Bell. The Square itself had once been a cattle market, a skating rink and at another time served as the place where the circus was held. The Square as we know it now dates back to 1901 when it was opened by Colonel Sadler. The Town Hall dominates this picture. The Prince and Princess of Wales opened the grand £130,000 building in 1889.

Left: A picture from 1972 showing the section of Linthorpe Road which was to be pedestrianised as part of the movement to create a more shopper-friendly central area. The contractors' sign on the left of the photograph indicates their aspirations for the Cleveland Centre. With 65 shop units, 12 boutiques and major stores such as Littlewoods, Tesco and Boots in the 'climate controlled malls' the new centre created much interest among the shoppers of Middlesbrough. Amidst all the new building work which, for a period of around a decade had shaped the heart of virtually every town centre in the land, a major corruption scandal hit the headlines when the Poulson inquiry began in July 1972. People reacted with sadness in May of the same year when news of the death of the Duke of Windsor, in Paris, was announced.

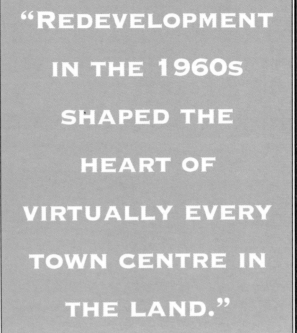

> "REDEVELOPMENT IN THE 1960s SHAPED THE HEART OF VIRTUALLY EVERY TOWN CENTRE IN THE LAND."

Below: Albert Road as it appeared around 1960. The view is dominated by the Corporation Hotel with its dark walls blackened by years of exposure to traffic fumes and the smoke from the domestic and industrial chimneys around Middlesbrough. The Corporation Hotel enjoyed a good reputation with the many guests who stayed there or attended any of the hundreds of functions it catered for over many decades. Ultimately though, its reputation was not enough to prevent it being pulled down in another rash of redevelopment aimed at bringing this part of town into the 'modern age.' Like so many other fine victorian buildings its place was soon taken by a multi-storey carpark.

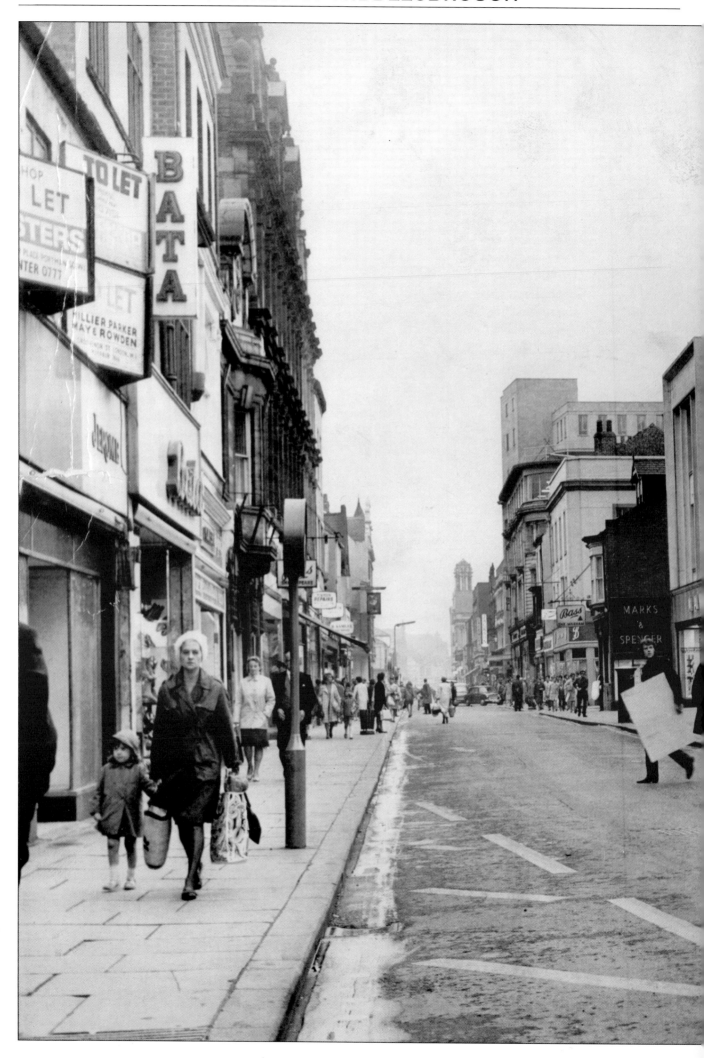

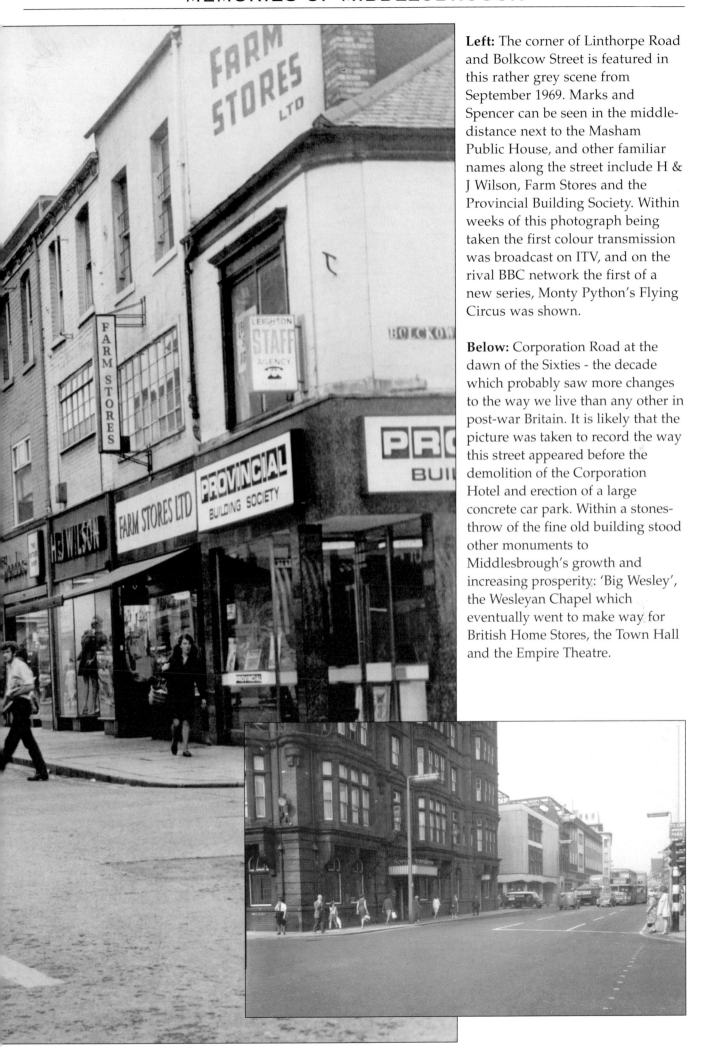

Left: The corner of Linthorpe Road and Bolckow Street is featured in this rather grey scene from September 1969. Marks and Spencer can be seen in the middle-distance next to the Masham Public House, and other familiar names along the street include H & J Wilson, Farm Stores and the Provincial Building Society. Within weeks of this photograph being taken the first colour transmission was broadcast on ITV, and on the rival BBC network the first of a new series, Monty Python's Flying Circus was shown.

Below: Corporation Road at the dawn of the Sixties - the decade which probably saw more changes to the way we live than any other in post-war Britain. It is likely that the picture was taken to record the way this street appeared before the demolition of the Corporation Hotel and erection of a large concrete car park. Within a stones-throw of the fine old building stood other monuments to Middlesbrough's growth and increasing prosperity: 'Big Wesley', the Wesleyan Chapel which eventually went to make way for British Home Stores, the Town Hall and the Empire Theatre.

Below: The failure of the traffic signals at the junction of Linthorpe Road and Borough Road resulted in this young policeman having to put on his white sleeve gaiters to perform point duty at the busy intersection outside the Midland Bank. Linthorpe Road is one of the oldest routes through Middlesbrough, as well, during most times of the town's development, as being one of the busiest. It has been an important thoroughfare for over a century and a half. Some of the 1960s motorcars add real character to the scene and are bound to bring back memories to those who drove them during this era.

Right: This picture dates from October 1967 and depicts the sturdy iron railings around the bus-bays where once passengers would queue for their bus after a busy day at work or at the shops. Middlesbrough's Exchange Bus Station was opened in 1925 and served several different bus companies, as well as thousands of their passengers, until being superseded by a new bus station in March 1931. The number of passengers grew rapidly as the population of the town expanded and began living further away from the centre. Trams had operated from a separate terminus and additional, though welcome, pressure was put upon the bus service when the trams finally ceased running in 1934.

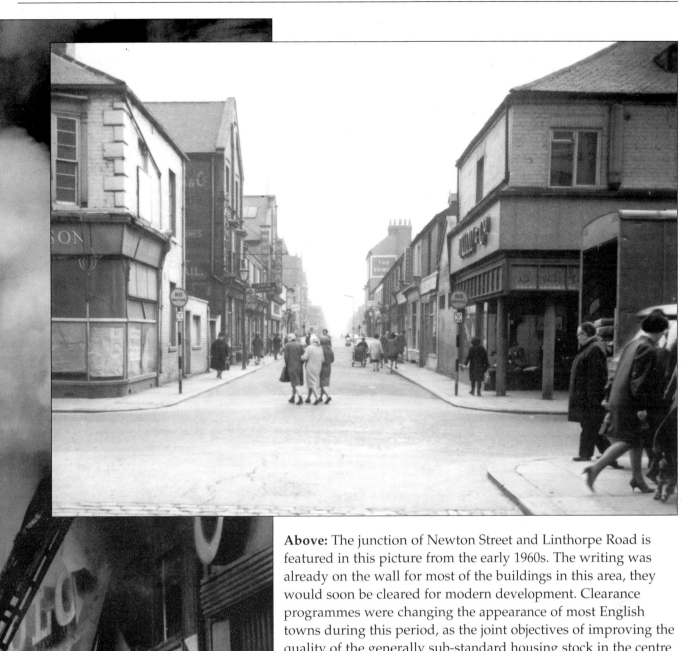

Above: The junction of Newton Street and Linthorpe Road is featured in this picture from the early 1960s. The writing was already on the wall for most of the buildings in this area, they would soon be cleared for modern development. Clearance programmes were changing the appearance of most English towns during this period, as the joint objectives of improving the quality of the generally sub-standard housing stock in the centre of town, and the pressure to create modern retail shopping areas took hold.

Left: Drama along Linthorpe Road in June 1969. A serious fire - one of the biggest blazes in the town centre for decades - caused the road to be closed for several hours as seven appliances from the Teesside Fire Brigade tackled the flames. Later, police officers investigated the cause of the fire which affected Spark's Cafe Royal and Dolcis shoe shop. Billowing smoke, the distinctive old-fashioned helmets worn by the firemen, and the huge, black Austin police car add a sense of drama and nostalgia in the scene. Middlesbrough has had more than her fair share of major town centre fires in the town centre. The worst of which was an arson attack caused by a 13 year-old firewood-seller in 1942 which destroyed many of the town's prominent retail premises.

Above: November 1963 was the date this picture was taken and a variety of 1960s cars add to the 'Sixties' feel created by it. This was already the age of concrete shops and office blocks in Middlesbrough, as evidenced by the properties seen here. In the same month that this local scene was captured the rest of the world was reeling after the the assasination of President Kennedy. A few months earlier, in August the audacious *Great Train Robbers* had captured the headlines with their robbery of a Mail Train and £1 million.

Right: The busy Linthorpe Road shopping area is featured in this picture which dates from June 1966. 'Alfie' was showing at the ABC Cinema on the right of the picture. The world of films and cinema was going through a difficult time when this picture was taken in the mid-1960s. The rise of the television age resulted in a decline in cinema audiences and an avalanche of cinema closures followed. At the same time, bingo halls became popular as a form of entertainment and gambling which appealed particularly to women. Many cinema buildings were saved by their conversion to bingo halls. 1966 will be remembered as the year when England rejoiced after their team won the world cup in a nail-biting match against West Germany at Wembley.

An interesting 1950s view of Newhouses corner and the Burtons tailors store opposite the famous local retail emporium. The sign in the Burtons window proclaims 'also at 118-132 New Oxford Street London'... and 'Experience... Merit.... Value.' The ornate lamp standard is worth a mention, how much nicer they were on the streets of the town than the bland concrete street lights which replaced them. Those readers with particularly good eyesight may be able to discern the sign indicating the location of Boots the chemists' shop, and the flag outside the property which promoted their film developing service. This would, have been black and white of course, and catered for the growing number of home photography enthusiasts and their Box-Brownies.

Right: The corner of Linthorpe Road and Corporation Road is seen in this late 1950s view, dominated by the bold exterior of British Home Stores. The well-known store stands on a site formerly occupied by the Wesley Chapel, on the corner of Linthorpe Road and Corporation Road, and known with great affection as "Big Wesley." The Chapel had been opened for the first time in September 1863 at the considerable cost, at the time, of £6,000. It could accommodate 840 worshippers, far in excess of the capacity necessary when it was pulled down in the mid 1950s.

Below: The recently-opened Middlesbrough Police Station as it appeared in December 1963. The modern lines and artistic cladding effect of the upper storeys were not to everyone's taste when the establishment opened. This picture suggests that the design was ahead of its time, it looks far more in-keeping with the style of buildings we are familiar with today, and the selection of motorcars seen parked along the adjacent streets looks quaintly out of date beside the modern station. The police station is located just a short walk away from the administrative and commercial heart of Middlesbrough, ideally suited to the needs of the growing town.

Wartime

Right: As part of the British Legion Festival of Remembrance this comedy sketch featuring "Old Bill" and "Young Bill" was popular with the audience that came to see them on November 13th 1949.

Below: As the clouds of war gathered around Europe, steps were taken in Britain to prepare the country in case Britain was drawn into conflict with the aggressive Nazi regime. In this picture several members of the 3rd A.A Division Signals Corps (T.A) are seen relaxing on the Hustler playing Fields close to the Drill Hall on Stockton Road. The picture dates from September 1939 but the Territorial Army Unit was formed in March 1939 and consisted mainly of G.P.O staff with Company Captain Baines, the senior area Telephone Engineer, being the officer in charge. Some of the names of the officers shown here are know. They are, left to right, Wilf Costello, "Gunner" Greenfield, Jack Illingworth, Arnold Hadfield, F. Mc Cabe, Les Ayres, an ATS girl, ...and other members of the Company.

This picture dates from around 1941 and features Middlesbrough's squad of "Gas Identification Officers." Here they pose for the photographer outside their local headquarters - St. Hilda's Lodge on Linthorpe Road, complete with their anti-gas suits which were designed to give the ultimate protection against all known forms of poisonous gas. At the time of the Second World War painful memories remained of the effect that gas attacks had caused in the trenches of France during the last conflict. The fear was that a similar deployment of gas from aircraft against the civilian population would cause mayhem. In the event there was never any enemy gas attack on British soil during the Second World War.

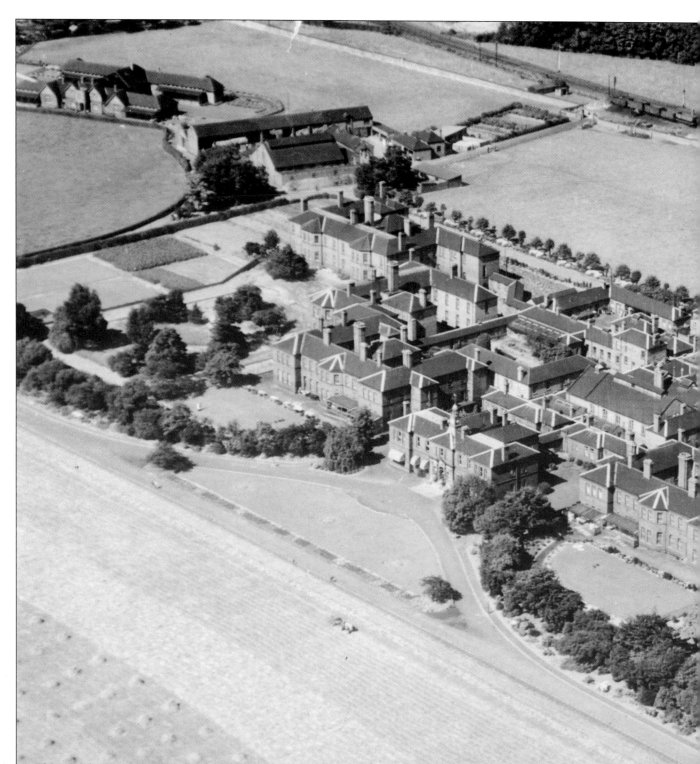

This aerial view was taken from an aeroplane flying at 2000 feet above St. Luke's Hospital. The picture dates from July 1951, just over half a century after the hospital had opened. St. Lukes catered for the needs of the mentally ill and was situated along Marton Road. This view gives an excellent impression of the delightful wooded surroundings, the farmland and the railway line in the background, all combining to provide a tranquil setting for those recovering from mental illness. It is interesting to note that the needs of the motor car were not as great as they are today, back in the early 1950s. There is no evidence of huge car parking areas (or even of small ones!) as there would be in a similar photograph of hospital grounds in modern times.

Bird's eye view

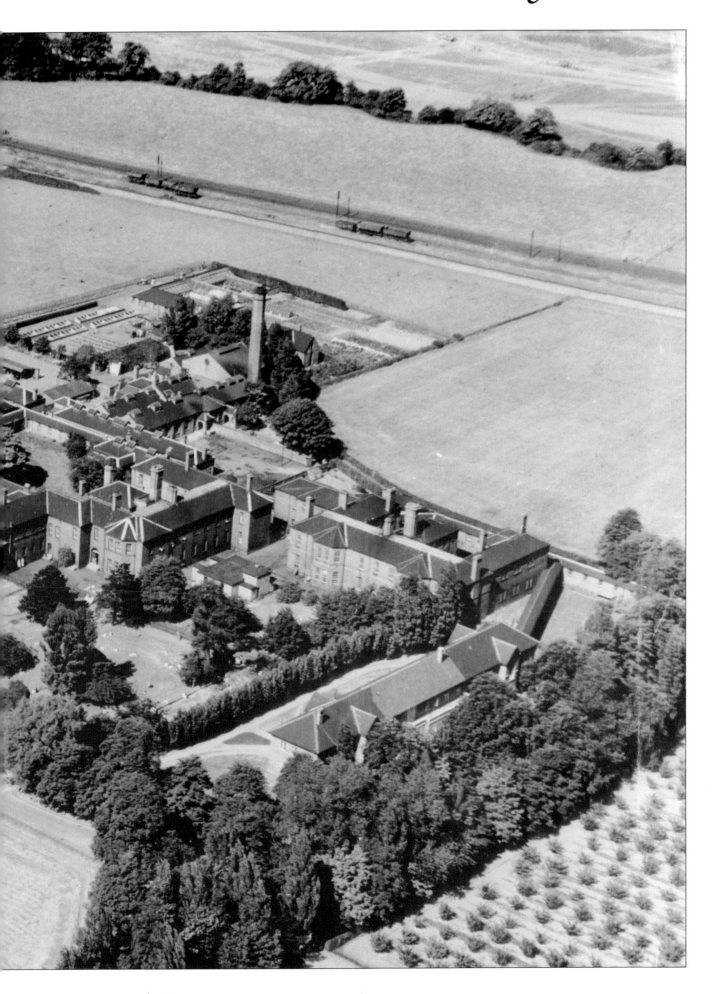

Rows of Victorian Terraced houses can be seen in this aerial view of the town. From a population of less than 200 people in 1830 the town grew rapidly in the following decades. The 'arrival' of the first blast furnace in the 1850s heralded the onset of a really serious period of growth. By 1860 the population had soared to close on 20,000 people. As the population grew so did the need to provide economical housing within reach of the workforce's place of employment. By 1880 there were over 55,000 people in the town and by 1910 this had almost doubled. The demand for affordable housing to accommodate the burgeoning population seemed relentless, as was the pressure to pack as many houses as possible into the land adjacent to the industrial areas.

"THE 'NEW' POLICE STATION WAS OPENED IN THE 1960S AND THE CONSTANTINE COLLEGE WAS OPENED IN 1930 BY HRH THE PRINCE OF WALES".

A photograph dating from 1969 showing Middlesbrough in the midst of the changes which would transform it. The angle of the camera gives a pleasing view of the heart of the town centre and the river beyond. The Furness Shipyard can be seen at the top right of the picture with the Cannon Street clearance area and St. Columbia's Church closer to the camera. The bottom-left of the picture contains a clear view of the Police Station and the Constantine College. This 'new' Police Station was opened in the 1960s and the Constantine College dates from 1930, having being opened by the Prince of Wales. The centre of the picture contains Middlesbrough's central shopping area.

A picture dating from 1969 showing the break up of the grid-iron pattern of streets for which the town was well-known. Clairville Sports Stadium can be seen at the top right of the scene. There is clear evidence of the re-development of the St. Hilda's district at the bottom of the photograph, and the erection of modern, concrete structures in the heart of the town. Nearer to the centre of the picture the Town Hall, along with the library building, new police station and Victoria Square are clearly visible.

Shopping spree

Below: Newhouse Corner in a picture dating from around 1930. The junction of Corporation Road and Linthorpe Road was a popular spot for shoppers. This picture was taken during the approach to Christmas - a clue being the 'Xmas Gifts' sign displayed in Newhouses' window. The Dickenson and Benson's store on the right was destroyed by fire in June 1942. Everyone is wearing a hat, despite their wealth or lack of it. Many were of the fashionable skull-hugging rounded variety where the ladies were concerned, and flat caps and 'homburgs' were popular with the gentlemen. Interestingly too, even some of the children in picture are wearing garments trimmed with fur - a fashion that would not find favour with today's public!

Right: This picture was taken in the hairdressing department of *Dickenson and Benson's* store on Linthorpe Road. This was a far cry from the modern hairdressing salons which are found up and down the high streets of every town in the country today. It was usual, in the *better class* establishments at least, for ladies to have their hair 'done' in individual booths. This was because an air of secrecy surrounded what went on between the hairdresser and the lady client concerned. In most cases the lady would never admit to having a particular kind of treatment, whether it be colouring or perming... not even to her closest friends. The equipment shown here - used to create an early permanent wave effect - looks like something out of a torture chamber in comparison to the modern forms of hair care we know.

Below: This imposing sight was Victoria Buildings, the headquarters of Middlesbrough's Co-operative Society for many years. The effect on the Co-op on the everyday lives of local people cannot be under-estimated. They would 'feed', 'furnish' and 'bury' the population in towns like Middlesbrough up and down the country and became involved in virtually every aspect of food production and retailing from farm to counter as the years progressed. This property was situated at the corner of Clifton Street, on the opposite side of Linthorpe Road to the *Gaumont* cinema. It was first opened at the turn of the century at a cost of £16,000. Sadly, 1942 saw the building badly damaged in an air-raid and the property was later completely redeveloped by the Co-op.

"MANY MIDDLESBROUGH FAMILIES WILL HAVE FOND MEMORIES OF VISITING NEWHOUSES STORE OVER THE YEARS."

Above: Newhouses Corner at the junction of Linthorpe Road. The now bustling retail area of Linthorpe Road originally served as the main link between the township of Middlesbrough and Linthorpe village. Newhouses store was something of an institution in the town and generations of Middlesbrough families will have fond memories of visiting it over the years. Later the company was taken over by the Debenhams organisation.

Above: Crowds of shoppers in the town on a busy Saturday. Middlesbrough's large department stores succeeded in attracting shoppers from far beyond the boundary of the town. Some of the big names in high street retailing have served the people of Middlesbrough for longer than most of us can remember; *Uptons,* of course, and *Binns,* originally founded in Sunderland in 1811, and trading from Middlesbrough since 1923. Two major fires destroyed earlier premises and they moved into their present location in 1953. They were taken over by the *House of Fraser* organisation in the mid-1950s. Older readers may have fond memories of *Dickenson and Benson* on Linthorpe Road, destroyed in Middlesbrough's worst case of arson, in 1942. In modern times bright new shopping centres add to the 'draw' of the local shopping environment - in Middlesbrough's case the Cleveland Centre leads the campaign.

Right: This publicity photograph was taken of the Co-operative Society's butcher's department window. The date is uncertain, but a sign in the window announces that it is part of a "National Co-operative Propaganda Campaign." A variety of meat was on offer, including mutton at 6d per pound, prime trapped rabbits and beef from the Argentine. Delightful.

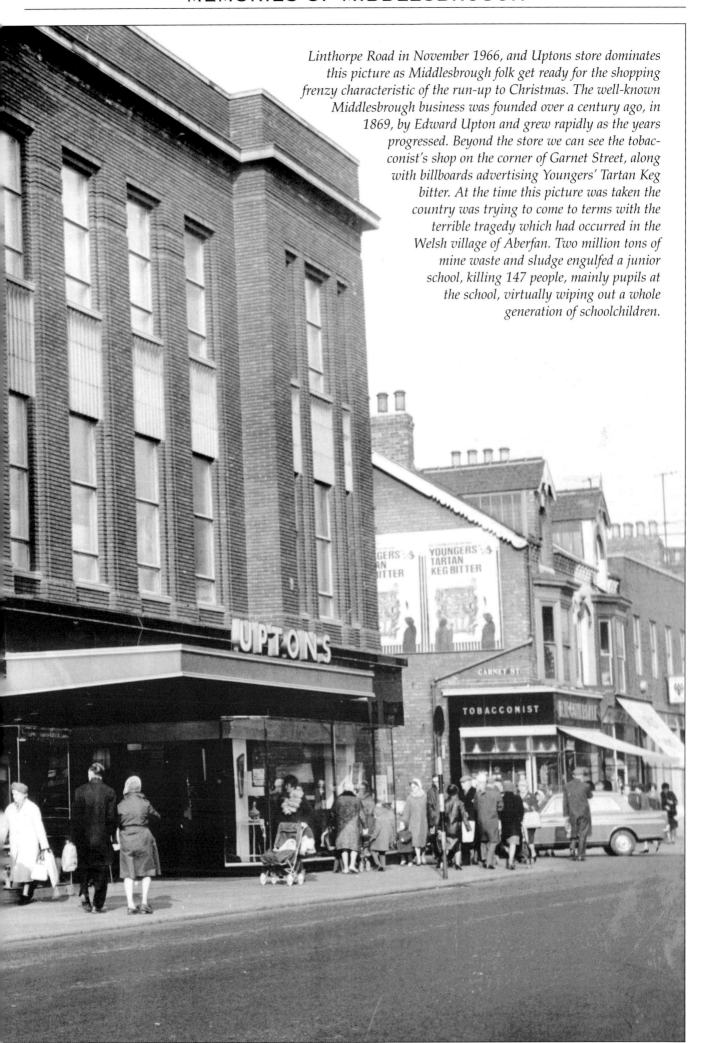

Linthorpe Road in November 1966, and Uptons store dominates this picture as Middlesbrough folk get ready for the shopping frenzy characteristic of the run-up to Christmas. The well-known Middlesbrough business was founded over a century ago, in 1869, by Edward Upton and grew rapidly as the years progressed. Beyond the store we can see the tobacconist's shop on the corner of Garnet Street, along with billboards advertising Youngers' Tartan Keg bitter. At the time this picture was taken the country was trying to come to terms with the terrible tragedy which had occurred in the Welsh village of Aberfan. Two million tons of mine waste and sludge engulfed a junior school, killing 147 people, mainly pupils at the school, virtually wiping out a whole generation of schoolchildren.

Right: The *British Home Stores* building dominates this picture from 23 July 1969. The Town Hall clock tower is on the left of the picture and a variety of 1960s motor cars adds colour to the scene. The location is of course, the busy corner of the Newport, Linthorpe and Corporation Roads. Before the British Home Stores building was constructed part of the site was occupied by the imposing brick-built Wesley chapel which had stood on the spot since 1863. Demolition came in the mid-1950s and the congregation relocated to Park Wesley Chapel.

Below: A familiar view of the *British Home Stores* building, taken before the company adopted the bright, modern logo which graces the store today. It stood beside the *York and County Savings Bank* and opposite *Burtons and Newhouses* - the reflections of both firms can just be seen in the *BHS* window. This picture dates from the early 1960s, the dawn of the 'consumer age' which was to transform the face of shopping for the next couple of decades. During this time determined efforts were made to separate the shopper on foot from the fumes and physical danger of motor traffic. It was the turning point in British retailing which saw the birth of many concrete shopping malls and multi-storey car parks. In terms of the effect this was to have on the appearance of the town centre Middlesbrough did better than most similar-sized towns in the same circumstances, many of which had the very heart and character ripped out of their traditional shopping and commercial centres.

At work

Below: Slightly over a hundred pensioners, all gentlemen of course, are seen gathered for this photograph. They are former employees of 'Smiths' and are seen outside the ship-builders premises. Smith's played an important role in the economic life of the town and provided employment for whole families at their shipbuilding yard. Unlike the case in modern times, it was typical to join a firm like Smith's as an apprentice, possibly on the introduction of one's father or brother, and always within days of leaving school, with the expectation of learning a trade and remaining in the employ of the company until retirement. Of course, in an industry like shipbuilding there was always the danger of being laid off when the order-book was thin or when economic slumps hit the country, but the principle of working for one employer for life, when work was available, was firmly established in the minds of the workforce.

Bottom: A most unusual photograph showing Middlesbrough in 1926. The scene was captured from the top of the Transporter Bridge and is unusual because the majority of the fifty or so chimneys are bereft of smoke. The reason was that a coal strike was in progress at the time, leaving the area unusually pollution-free. The photograph roughly represents the half-way stage on the scale of Middlesbrough's development, from her earliest industrial steps to modern times. Most of the elements of the town's industrial strength can be seen here - iron and steel working, coal, the railways and, of course, a thriving port. These were the foundations upon which her future prosperity would be built.

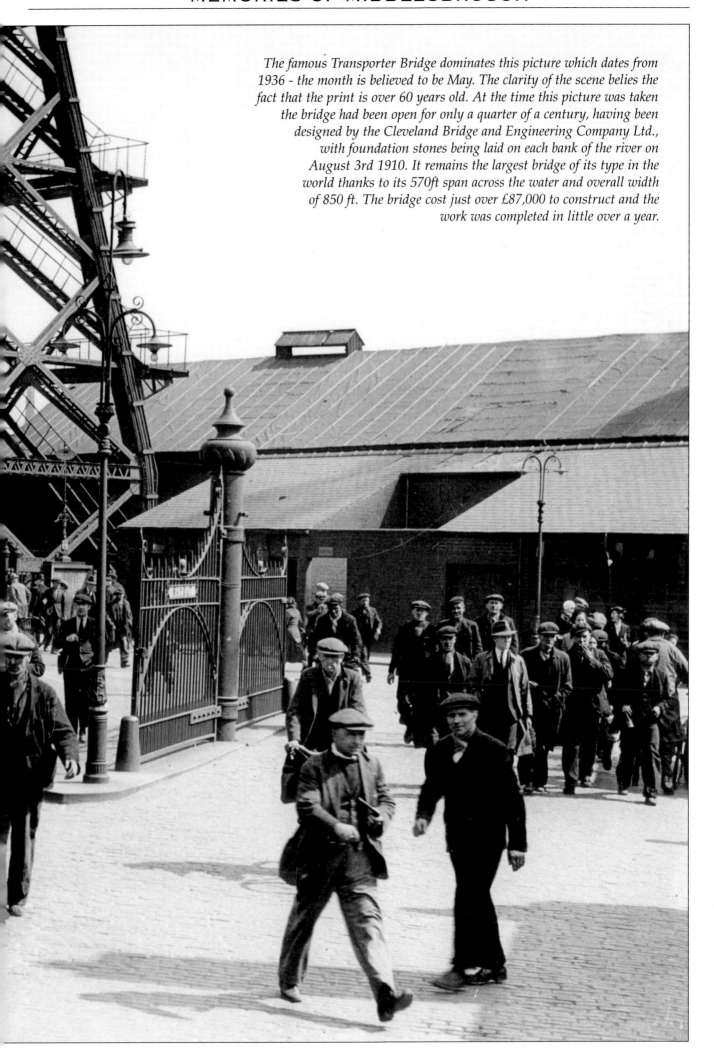

The famous Transporter Bridge dominates this picture which dates from 1936 - the month is believed to be May. The clarity of the scene belies the fact that the print is over 60 years old. At the time this picture was taken the bridge had been open for only a quarter of a century, having been designed by the Cleveland Bridge and Engineering Company Ltd., with foundation stones being laid on each bank of the river on August 3rd 1910. It remains the largest bridge of its type in the world thanks to its 570ft span across the water and overall width of 850 ft. The bridge cost just over £87,000 to construct and the work was completed in little over a year.

Left: Unloading an ore-carrier on the South Bank Wharf was a fairly routine activity, but one cannot fail to be impressed by the size of the machinery involved in the task as featured in this photograph. The picture dates from the early 1960s, a time when Middlesbrough Dock had over 2000 yards of quays. The water in the dock had a surface area of more than 24 acres, but even these impressive statistics were not enough to ensure the survival of the facility. Eventually it was agreed that the capacity of the dock was insufficient to cater for modern needs and it closed to commercial traffic in 1980. The Tees Dock then took on the role formerly performed by the Middlesbrough Dock from its location near Lackenby.

Above: Smith's Dock was the scene of this launching which took place around 1960. Ship building went hand-in-hand with the adjacent iron and steel industries. The Smith's Dock Company had been established in 1899, formed by the merger of three Tyneside shipyards, T & W Smith and Co., H.S. Edwards and Sons, and Edwards Brothers. The company could justify its claim to have been involved in the ship building industry since 1768 - more than 20 years before the French Revolution! Shipbuilding activities were undertaken by the company in Teesside from 1908. The shipyard played an important role in wartime as well as making an invaluable contribution to the local economy by providing employment and supporting countless other smaller businesses in the region. Sadly, Smith's ceased their shipbuilding activities in the area in the 1980s.

Almost a century of St. Mary's confident commitment

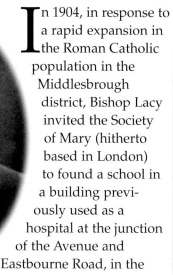

In 1904, in response to a rapid expansion in the Roman Catholic population in the Middlesbrough district, Bishop Lacy invited the Society of Mary (hitherto based in London) to found a school in a building previously used as a hospital at the junction of the Avenue and Eastbourne Road, in the village of Linthorpe. The first short-lived headmaster was Fr. Watters who felt the school was doomed to fail and he was superseded in 1906 by Fr. Moran.

The school grew very slowly. By 1910 St Mary's, now with Father Moran in charge, had only 67 pupils. Father Moran was undaunted and organised a full programme for the pupils he did have, complete with Prize-giving and Sports Day. The school was loyally supported by the clergy and parish. Most North Riding boys came on 'Bishop's Scholarships' and not many pupils paid full fees. Numbers began to grow. By 1918 a total of 100 boys was reached, some of them boarders, and by 1920 there were 160 day boys, 20 boarders and the school was only £500 in the red at the bank.

At the beginning of the First World War the school had to close until its cellars had been reinforced to make them into safe air-raid shelters. Because the school had Direct Grant status, no government grants were available for this.

In 1922 Father William Fox became headmaster. He knew the school well, having been an assistant master for 14 years. More and more pupils continued to arrive and the need for extra classrooms had been met by the acquisition of several army huts in 1919. They had good use made of them on Saturdays for extra classes in woodwork, art, shorthand and music.

In 1923 the school's catchment area was increased. The Bishop was quietly using it as a junior seminary, and successfully, judging by the number of old boys who entered the priesthood.

By the thirties most pupils were accommodated in a large house. Behind this was the school gymnasium. A row of huts which separated two paved areas were still being used. One tree on the area required for the paved yard was so venerable that instructions were given to pave around it. Beyond the buildings was the playing field.

Soon a single storey building was put up on

Above: The College in Grange Road.
Top left: Fr. James Moran, S.M., the 'real founder' of St Mary's College, Middlesbrough.
Left: The staff as seen in 1927.

increased again so, inevitably, there were more huts. Building began again on an adjacent site.

In the schools' reorganisation of the early 1970s, St Mary's became a co-educational sixth form college. The management hoped that the spirit of its past would prevail. At first the girls from the Convent and the boys from St Mary's were in two opposing camps, but in their self-imposed blue denim uniforms the two groups soon merged, worked together and endured together the 1975/76 modernisation when lorries and mobile cranes trundled past classroom windows.

the old playing field which provided specialist rooms for art, chemistry and physics. When a new church was built, the old one became a general-purpose building. New playing fields were acquired out at Saltersgill, where pupils had to change in a draughty old cabin.

After the war, academic results improved and numbers increased. School dinners and school milk made their appearance. At this time, St Mary's lost its Direct Grant status and became 'voluntary assisted'. The local authority was generous in supplying equipment.

A new college building was begun on the playing fields at Saltersgill. Classes moved out there as rooms became available. Since the two buildings were more than a mile apart, putting together the timetable became a nightmare. The school roll

Since then St. Mary's has increased in stature. It is now Middlesbrough's only sixth form college and

has acquired a justified reputation for academic excellence. The Chief Executive of the Further Education Funding Council visited the college after reading its impressive inspection report. In a letter to the Principal, he wrote, "I was impressed by the confident commitment of both staff and pupils."

Above: Phase one of the new college, built on playing fields at Saltersgill.
Top left: A delightful picture of the school library taken in the 1930s.
Left: Another staff photo-graph, this time taken in 1955.

The sight of a ship being launched is always awe-inspiring, no matter how many times the event has been witnessed. The culmination of months or years of hard work, the sheer mass of the vessel concerned as she slips slowly and smoothly into the river is enough to set the pulse racing of even the most casual observer. Shipbuilding had been going on at Smith's Dock since shortly before the start outbreak of the First World War. This dramatic picture, taken in 1951, captures the moment that the newly-built Athelfoam slid into the water for the first time, much to the relief of the excited spectators.

2858.

Above: The mighty *Lustrous* slides down the slipway towards the cold river from Smith's Dock. The vessel was covered in bunting and flags in recognition of the celebrations which were associated with any successful launch, and tugs were waiting to shepherd the partly-completed vessel just a few yards away on the river. As the ship slid away towards the water it revealed the long stairway which had provided access to the workers who had laboured on the vessel, seen here on the right of the picture.

"SADLY, MIDDLESBROUGH DOCK COULD NOT COPE WITH THE CHANGING TIMES AND CLOSED IN 1980."

Below: This picture was taken in May 1966 and shows the cargo vessel *Benhope* being unloaded at Middlesbrough Dock. The dock dates back to 1842 and was constructed to replace the coal shipping staithes at Port Darlington. It had been found that these were inadequate to cope with the increasing size of visiting ships which required deeper water in order to dock at the port. Sadly, Middlesbrough Dock itself eventually could not cope with the changing times and it closed in 1980. The regions' shipping would later be catered for by Tees Dock and Teesport which are closer to the North Sea. During the year this scene was captured, Freddie Laker formed his cut-price transatlantic airline and the Labour Party won a landslide victory in the General Election. Interestingly, on the very day before this picture was taken, Myra Hindley and Ian Brady received life sentences after being found guilty of the "Moors Murders."

Construction work was well under way in 1932 on The Tees (Newport) Bridge which dominated this section of the river for over sixty years. The statistics relating to the unusual but effective structure are breathtaking; 8,000 tons of steel and 750 tons of cast iron were required by contractors, Dorman Long, along with over three times that weight (28,000 tons) of concrete. The lifting span alone weighed over 1500 tons and could travel 99 feet skywards to allow river traffic to pass beneath it. Since November 1990 this part of the bridge has been firmly fixed at its lowest level to allow road traffic to pass through.

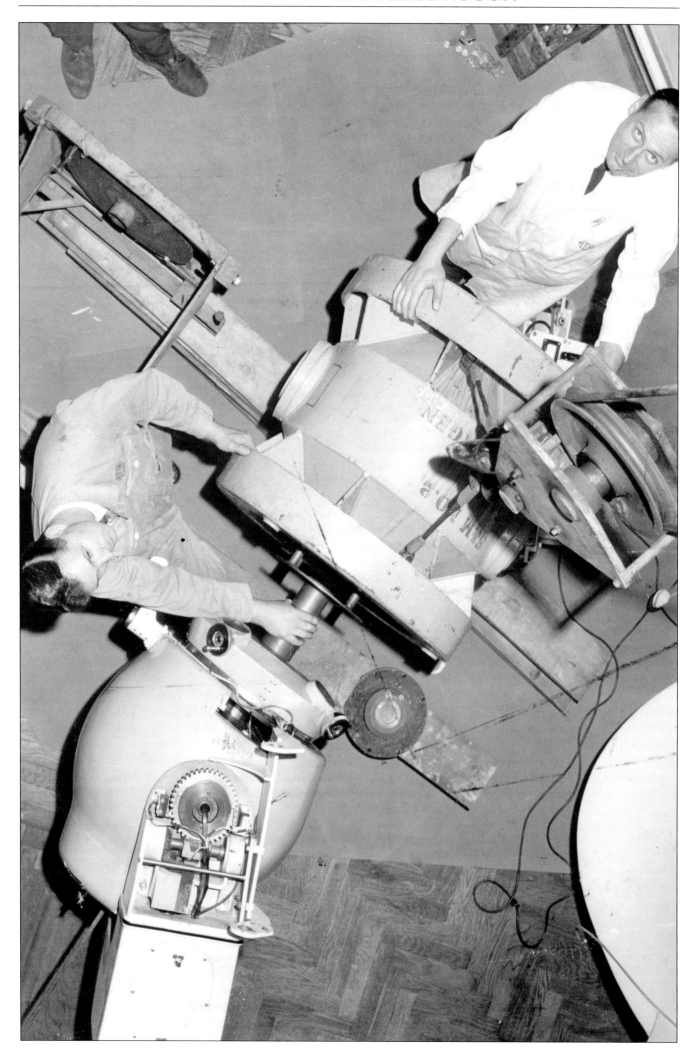

Above: This was the nerve-centre of Middlesbrough's Police Headquarters as it appeared in October 1962. In comparison to the hi-tech world of police communications in modern times this scene looks very dated. This was slightly before the dawn of the age when every foot patrol was linked to the control-centre by a two way radio - and in the days when the wireless set in each patrol car took up a sizeable portion of the boot. The two young men on the left of the picture wear badges denoting their status as police cadets. Where are they now, we wonder?

Left: This dramatic photograph from 1967 shows the installation of a new radioactive capsule in the "Cobalt Bomb" Unit at North Ormesby Hospital, Middlesbrough. Part of the roof of the building had to be removed in the delicate three-hour operation in the treatment room as the tiny radioactive source was replaced. The unit, which specialised in the treatment of cancer patients, was opened in 1962 after a successful public appeal for £30,000. The picture shows the two-ton casing which housed the device being lowered carefully into position. North Ormesby Hospital was built in 1861 and served the people of the area for 120 years until its demolition in 1981. When built it was financed by local subscriptions, mainly from local dignitaries and factory owners, which covered the £2650 cost of the work. Initially the hospital was very small, with only 25 beds.

> "NORTH ORMESBY HOSPITAL WAS OPENED IN 1861 AND SERVED THE PEOPLE OF THE AREA FOR 120 YEARS BEFORE DEMOLITION IN 1981."

Uptons - business success for television pioneers

In 1869, a certain Mr Edward Upton came from East Bridgeford in Nottinghamshire, where he had earned his living as a market gardener, to start a small grocery business in South Bank-on-Tees. In those days the site of the later premises in Nelson Street was just green fields.

The firm developed steadily and, in the late 1890s, Mr Walter Upton, later to become Chairman of the Board of Directors, and Mr Martin Upton took over management of the company. They opened four new branches and extended the business to include cycles, furniture and musical instruments. Later still, a shop was opened at Bennett's Corner for the sale of pianos, music and organs.

About that time, Mr Upton started a system of 'Payment out of Income', now universally known as hire-purchase, so becoming the pioneer of HP trading on Teesside.

In the late 1920s Messrs Edward and Walter Upton became Joint Governing Directors and business continued to prosper, benefiting from the solid foundation laid by the first Mr Upton.

In Middlesbrough the original premises were in Newport Crescent and were opened in 1907. In 1920, larger premises were taken at 156, Linthorpe Road. Later in that year, 175, Linthorpe Road was taken over and these premises were enlarged in 1933, 1936 and 1938. Until the fire that gutted this main store in 1942, its corner site was a landmark in Middlesbrough.

Meanwhile, expansion in other directions was going on. The Radio Service Depot in Southfield Road was opened in 1936 and was later expanded several times. New depots were opened in Stockton and Darlington to cope with the overflow of work from the main depot. Every opportunity was taken to acquire technical knowledge in the fields of cycling, furniture, radio and television.

From the early days of television, Uptons pioneered many experiments and men with national reputations in the field of television started in the firm's radio department.

As early as 1938, in a little wooden hut on the edge of the moors, near the village of Ormesby, a small party

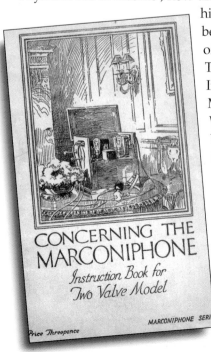

CONCERNING THE MARCONIPHONE
Instruction Book for Two Valve Model

MARCONIPHONE SERIE

Price Threepence

Above: *Mr Walter Upton Snr and his wife in 1920*

persuaded the Company to establish it early in 1938. Five minutes after the set was switched on in February, pictures could be seen. Only a year before reception had been confined to a 20 mile radius round Alexandra Palace. Edward Upton knew that the isolated position of the Company's station was responsible for its success. However, this by no means meant television for everyone in the district. The famous 70 minute programme had been transmitted to Middlesbrough on a particularly favourable day to a special set at a great height. Nevertheless, the BBC requested full details of the Uptons' experiment and regular reports on Mr Sowerby's further experiments.

of men received television pictures which were being transmitted from the BBC TV station 220 miles away at Alexandra Palace in London. This was the greatest distance from the station that pictures had ever been received. The party at Ormesby saw a 70-minute programme, part of it with perfect reception, using a standard £100 commercial set, slightly adjusted. Best receiving conditions were ensured by using a special aerial and a special location for the mast 700 feet above sea level, well removed from trees and houses, in a direct line with the transmitter. The setting-up of the station was the responsibility of Mr G Sowerby who was the wireless manager at Uptons. He had

The station, at the top of Gypsy Lane, was a maze of intricate apparatus besides the actual television set augmented with a two-valve unit.

Above: Jack Houseman one of the pre war drivers.
Below: The radio and television service fleet in 1965.

decisions made at Directors' meetings reached workers through Branch Managers and Heads of Departments. Similarly, ideas and suggestions from workers travelled in reverse order to the Directors. By 1951, staff were being invited to share in profits, in management and, if they wished, in shareholding. A leaflet sent out in 1954 to all 'very good previous customers' advertised the full range of available ware, furniture, carpets and bedding, fabrics, kitchenware, nursery goods, cycles and motor cycles, television, radio and

By 1944, when E Upton & Sons Ltd introduced their 'Co-partnership and Profit Sharing Scheme', the company was established at 32, Southfield Road and had branches at South Bank, Billingham, Darlington, Redcar, Stockton and North Ormesby. Literature explaining the scheme was distributed to all the staff. A booklet included a diagram showing how domestic appliances, all supplied and fitted by factory trained technicians and craftsmen.

Top: The new extension to the store when it was opened in 1962.
Above left: Uptons store following the fire in 1942.

Government regulations to control trade prevented the Company offering no-deposit credit but this was allowed to established customers on a gradual payment account if it was settled within nine months.

Custom was encouraged through a household account to be settled in 30 weeks. This latter scheme offered credit on goods to a value ranging between thirty shillings and 25 pounds with a deposit of two shillings in the pound. Weekly payments could be made at any branch with allowances for early settlement. There was also a free car service to any of the company's showrooms for out-of-town customers on request.

Mr Ronald Trenter took over policy decisions in 1995 and business is now flourishing. Recently the company has been able to open a new store in Hartlepool and also to take over the Binns' store in Scunthorpe.

The company's current trading policy is to sell affordable clothing and household merchandise to middle-income wage earners on Teesside, backed by superior standards of housekeeping and service in a friendly environment. Many of Uptons' customers are from families who have shopped with them for decades.

Even though Uptons has a long history, the company is constantly looking into the future. In the last eighteen months it has opened a new store in Hartlepool, aquired another in Scunthorpe and at present is actively searching for a couple of stores per year to add to the exsiting stores. By the year 2000, the company hopes to have doubled its size. Along with this, the company promises exciting new products and services for the new millennium. The new look Uptons is ready for the next century.

Above: Staff in period costume help to celebrate the stores centenery.
Left: Alastair Pirrie, the Radio Tees DJ, provides entertainment at the opening of the new store in Stockton in 1972.

A business built on personal service

To capitalise on the post World War I boom, Ernest Oswald Race, who was always referred to by his middle name, (Ossie), founded his furniture business in 1920, following his de-mob from the Green Howards with whom he had served since 1912. He was born in Butterknowle, County Durham in 1890 and on leaving school in 1904 he worked for Eatons Furniture Shop in Sussex Street, Middlesbrough, where he became manager in 1911.

After the war he decided to set up on his own and converted the downstairs of the family house into a shop, commencing in 1920. Most of the stock was second-hand furniture, plus hardware, carpets, rugs and linoleum. The shop continued in this way until the outbreak of war in 1939. Meanwhile, son Clive,

who was born in 1921, began an apprenticeship with Binns in the carpet and linoleum department, until 1940 when he joined the RAF, serving in the Far East as a wireless operator. After de-mobilisation in May 1946, Clive joined the family

business and it was a very difficult period for trading. Not much new furniture was manufactured during the war years and even then was only obtainable with dockets. It took many years for things to return to normal.

Sadly, Ossie Race died in June 1953, leaving his wife, Beatrice. Clive carried on the business, buying the property, and in 1959 purchased the next door premises at 170 Borough Road. In 1960 the first shop front was constructed and internal alterations and improvements were made.

In 1956 the first Race For Furniture Bedford CF Van was purchased and a continual personal delivery service has ensued ever since. Clive's wife, Leah worked in the business, both in selling and clerical, which in those days was mainly selling new carpets, floor coverings and furniture.

During the early 1970s, the Council made a compulsory purchase order on half the block in Borough Road - a blow in terms of its valuation, and Clive fought the Council and won against the compulsory purchase order. Times were very hard, many properties were left empty and became derelict and the business suffered greatly.

In 1978, Grandson Iain Clive Race, who was born in 1957, joined the company after working in London and immediately a new larger van was purchased. The company continued to grow steadily until 1987 when the shop front was extended forward, modernised and many internal improvements were made.

From this point the company really accelerated, stocking a wider variety of furniture and moving more upmarket in the products sold.

1991 saw Clive retiring from the business and in 1992, Kenneth Lord, who had started work there in 1981, was appointed as manager, looking after the daily running of the business.

A huge period of growth ensued to keep apace with fierce competition in the retail furniture business on Teesside. Advertising was extensive, a large warehouse was acquired and further major extensions took place to the building. There is now a huge choice of quality furniture for the home on display, including suites, chairs, recliners, electric beds and chairs, beds, bedroom, dining and occasional furniture and accessories including lamps, pictures and mirrors.

In 1996 another branch was opened on the Skippers Lane Industrial Estate called 'The Pine Warehouse', specialising in solid pine furniture. At the same time, Race For Furniture had four extra warehouses purpose built and a

A "Cotswold" Three-Piece Suite covered in an attractive Tapestry, Rayon or Uncut Moquette, comprising Model 9 Settee and two Model 9a Easy Chairs. The backs and seats are sprung with patent sprung units and the arms are also sprung.

further larger van was also acquired. The staff increased to 30 and after the huge success of The Pine Warehouse, this branch was moved in October 1997 to a 10,000 square feet shop at Portrack Lane in Stockton. Also here, a third subsidiary of Race For Furniture was formed called 'The Leather Suite Centre', becoming the largest showroom in the North East of purely leather suites, and further expansion ideas are in the pipeline.

Race For Furniture still prides itself on old fashioned personal service, mixed with quality furniture and attention to detail. A unique and well-known feature is the free courtesy car that collects customers who have difficulty in getting out of their home to visit the various shops.

As the millennium approaches, the people of Middlesbrough and Teesside are still saying, as they did in the 1920s, "Let's Race For Furniture".

Above: A catalogue from the 1950s. A settee such as the one on the left would have cost about £12 4s. ***Below left:*** *Some of the staff in 1995. From left to right: Kenneth Lord, Colin Graydon, Clive Race, Geoff Blakey, Linda Bell, Iain Race, Keith Robinson, Barbara Boal, Kevin Steel and Leah Race.* ***Below:*** *The shop as it looks today.* ***Opposite page top left:*** *Ernest Oswald Race and son, Arthur, outside the shop in 1930.* ***Opposite page bottom left:*** *Clive Oswald Race outside the shop at the age of 12.* ***Opposite page top right:*** *The shop in 1951.* ***Opposite page below right:*** *Clive and Leah Race with their Bedford van in 1957*

The Cleveland Shopping Centre - Middlesbrough's own 'Endeavour'

In November 1961 a property developer, Norbert Sharland, with whom Leslie Furness had carried out several successful schemes, suggested a visit to Middlesbrough to assess the possibilities of redevelopment on a major scale. Neither were intimate with the area so they spent many hours walking the town, watching the pedestrian flow, debating the merits of working on one site rather than another.

The main shopping thoroughfare was found to be so well established that redevelopment away from this central core would have been foolish. The two men decided on the area bounded by Linthorpe Road, Bottomley Street, Fletcher Street and Fallows Street which seemed a typical 'natural' area for shopping renewal and extension, absorbing the less valuable parts to the rear of Linthorpe Road to compensate for some of the very expensive property that would need to be purchased on Linthorpe Road itself. Thus the established pedestrian flow through Newton Street would be maintained on redevelopment.

A meeting was held with the Borough Engineer and Surveyor. Messrs Sharland and Furness had already investigated carefully the commercial and social requirements and made detailed financial plans to fund the projected work. It was time to call in the architects. They appointed Messrs Turner, Lansdowne, Holt and Partners, then, in the following year, set about private negotiations with the current owners for the properties they would need to acquire.

Backers needed

Within a few months they had negotiated contracts to buy several important properties. Now they needed to 'sell' their idea for development to a finance company willing to lend the estimated £3 million needed to make it happen. In due course an

investment company, Barratt-Victoria (Middlesbrough) Property Company Ltd was formed.

Barratt-Victoria had a strong team. Their architects were sensitive to what would blend well with the surrounding area of town. They were also sensible enough to produce ideas that could be afforded financially and experienced enough to cope with all the constructional problems. It was expected that rebuilding would begin within 2 to 3 years.

The Borough Engineer and Surveyor approved the plans submitted in April 1962 but wanted the scheme enlarged to include Albert Road. His suggestion was incorporated and then the scheme was further enlarged to co-ordinate with plans to rebuild between Wesley Street and Fallows Street. By March 1963, therefore, the Arndale Property Trust submitted plans for a mammoth £10 million scheme stretching from Borough Road to

Left and above: The demolition of existing shops, which began in July 1969 to make way for the Cleveland Shopping Centre. Below: Construction begins in earnest and the first phase incorporating the Linthorpe Road perimeter shops is opened in 1970.

Corporation Road. Perhaps feeling that the idea had grown too big, Barratt-Victoria submitted a third scheme and consultants were appointed to make the decision.

After several meetings, it was decided that Barratt-Victoria and Arndale would each proceed independently to develop the sites each owned but all in conformity with the recommendations of the consultant surveyors. This co-operation seemed sensible since the substantial ownership of property already established would involve the minimum use of compulsory purchase powers.

However, it was not to be. The council decided it wished to deal with a single company or consortium as developer and wanted unified ownership of the whole area. At this stage Arndale decided not to pursue the scheme they had submitted the previous year.
Compulsory purchase
It was not until the summer of 1965, after Turner, Lansdowne, Holt & Partners had produced several variations on their

plans that the council felt able to agree in principle to the scheme. The redevelopment area now extended to six acres. The council intended to become the ground landlord but private enterprise would acquire by agreement the multitude of other property interests. Public roads ran through the site which would have to be closed and so it now became necessary to compulsorily acquire the land.

This involved exacting and time-consuming procedures under the Town and Country planning act. Numerous detailed plans were prepared, together with documents and reports. It was almost Christmas 1966 before the local authority formally submitted their proposals to the Minister of Housing and Local Government.

The public enquiry was held in September 1967. A public exhibition had been held previously and affected traders had been promised rehousing in the scheme with continuity of trading wherever possible. There were therefore few objections and the Minister's approval was given in 1968.

Promises to traders were kept. For example, the old Erimus public house was not demolished before new licensed premises were put up for Vaux Breweries and the National Westminster Bank was temporarily rehoused.

Building operations eventually started in July 1969. Six streets made way for the Cleveland Centre but these were not forgotten. The top half of Fletcher Street became the entrance to the centre for service vehicles to the first floor, and for shoppers' cars going to the second floor parking area. Two of the climate-controlled shopping malls have been named after Newton and Wesley Streets.

The seventies
The original development took ten years from conception to completion at a cost of four million pounds. Construction was in three phases, the first opening in 1970 and covering some Linthorpe Road perimeter shops. In 1972 the 2nd phase began with the opening of Newton Mall for the benefit of one shop. However, others quickly followed. At the end of the 3rd phase in 1973 there were 318,000 square feet of retail in a total 494,180 square feet.
The Legal and General Assurance Company purchased the Centre.

The eighties
By the early 80s it was clear that the Centre had become outdated through normal wear and tear and changes of legislation concerning fire, health and safety.

Legal and General appointed Bradshaw, Rowse and Harker as architects for the refurbishment programme carried out during 1984-6. It added 7,000 square feet of new retail space at a cost of more than £7 million. The Centre then consisted of 86 units incorporating a wine bar, restaurants, a roof top night club, three office blocks, a very large Health Centre and a car park with 550 spaces, leased to the local authority.

And today
In 1997 Legal and General again commissioned Bradshaw, Rowse and Harker to give the Centre a cosmetic uplift to the value of £3.5 million. This involved laying new floors throughout which gave a much lighter appearance. This was further improved by the provision of new ceilings with incorporated lighting.

Cladding and other new wall finishes were added, together with new signs and graphics to reflect the Centre's modern image. Improvements were made to most of the entrances and the area known as Cleveland Square was completely revamped, drawing all eyes to the main focal point, a fifth scale model of Captain Cook's ship, The Endeavour. Wall graphics depict a sea-scape and harbour scene and an attractive new feature is a map of one of Cook's voyages, set in the floor and lit by fibre optics.

The Centre identifies itself closely with Cleveland's most famous son. Maybe it is not unreasonable to suppose that a 20th Century Captain Cook would be proud to identify with the Cleveland Centre!

Above and left: Artist's impressions of the renovations which took place at the beginning of 1997, showing the replica of the Endeavour and the proposed new look for the entrance.
Facing page, top: A gala in the early 1980s passes the Cleveland Centre.
Facing page, bottom: A promotion in the 1990s, with the 'Spice Grills', the latest offering from Newboulds the Bakers.

Happy end to the Hill Street blues

In the late seventies the Middlesbrough press were told that the Council had sanctioned a prestigious £3 million development for the Hill Street site which would include two large stores, 60 smaller shops, covered and open markets and even cinemas and squash courts. Unfortunately, the announcement did not mean that work would start immediately. Wrangling over the financing of the project forced the Co-op to pull out but the situation was saved when Fine Fare announced that it would take over.

In 1980, Middlesbrough MP, Arthur Bottomley helped to get the Hill Street Centre project rolling by laying the foundation stone. Just three years later the tape was cut to mark the beginning of trading in a massive new extension that joined Debenhams' store to Hill Street.

The opening of the Hill Street Centre was the biggest shopping event in Middlesbrough in 1982. It had been open to the public for 12 months when the Mayor of Middlesbrough that year, Councillor Charles Godfrey led the official opening ceremony. Representatives from Middlesbrough's twin towns, Oberhausen in Germany and Dunkirk in France attended, together with Arthur Bottomley. Shopping malls were named after all three. The malls, known until then as East, South and West, became Oberhausen Mall, Dunkerke Mall and Bottomley Mall respectively.

A plaque was unveiled at the centre's 'christening'. It records that the centre was developed by French-Kier Property Investments and the Sun Alliance Insurance Group in association with Middlesbrough Council.

Councillor Godfrey held up the centre as one of the features of which the whole of Cleveland could be proud.Before the centre was opened Cleveland people had had to go south to Leeds or north to Newcastle to do major shopping. Now they only had to go to Middlesbrough.

Twenty five years before, in the late fifties, the area now occupied by the centre had been covered with

Below: This 1977 elevated view of the Hill Street site prior to redevelopment illustrates why the area was known as the 'North's biggest car park'. Within two years the building work had begun.

shops themselves. Their owners were more than willing to move in, investing literally millions of pounds at a time when retail trade was depressed. At the opening Councillor Godfrey was careful to thank executives from the store group for their confidence in pouring money into Middlesbrough at a time of general gloom over cutbacks and loss of jobs. Successful trading had been going on for a whole year at a time when the major industrial base for Cleveland had been rocked by large-scale redundancies.

The very large unit originally taken on by Fine Fare and subsequently occupied by other major supermarket retailers has recently been split into several smaller units which is generally considered to be a better use of the available space. Otherwise, the centre's history since its opening has been uneventful, and all the better for that. As the present manager says, "All we've done here is get on with the job."

back to back housing that stretched almost as far as Stockton. Its transformation was a tribute to a vast amount of dedicated hard work over a ten year period by the Council and the developers, French-Kier who had to battle their way through a series of obstacles. These certainly did not include the

Above: Hillbert the mascot flying high for Hill Street.
Above Left: Centre Manager D. White with lucky competition winners. Below: Majorettes take a breather during the Telethon which was held in the centre.

Geo. Humphreys - from lead paint to leader in its field

When George Humphreys set up his painting and decorating business on April 4th 1922 at 18, St Aidan's Street, his methods and materials were rather different from the ones his company employs today. The paint he used was mixed by hand and consisted of white lead, linseed oil, driers, turpentine and stainers.

Because of the lead content, one of Mr Humphreys' expenses was for medical examination of himself and any employees in accordance with the 'Employment in Lead Processes Act of 1920'.

Contract number Two, dated April 20th that year, for a Mrs. Jones of Victoria Road was for "Stripping Ceiling & Walls & Papering same, Staining & Varnishing woodwork" in one room. Humphreys supplied the materials and the total cost for the job amounted to £4 and five shillings.

Working from home
Mr Humphreys had formerly been a foreman painter and decorator at Smith's Dock, South Bank. Based at his home premises. By 1935 Mr Humphreys

was employing eight assistants. He was taking £2 ten shillings as a weekly wage. Messrs Bland and Coulthard were earning almost as much whilst the rest were possibly apprentices since they earned between fifteen shillings and twopence and eight shillings and threepence.

During the Second World War George continued his wallpapering and painting whilst his sons fought for their country, Fred in the RAF and Ken in the Royal Navy. He evidently did a good job because there was work for his two sons who re-joined him in the business, along with Bill Taylor.

After the Second World War
By 1947, in June of that year, the firm was working for a Miss McDonald. His estimate for decorating a whole house in Linthorpe Road amounted to £23 fifteen shillings. Miss McDonald was offered advice free of charge. "The present white woodwork in the house will have to be burnt off if brush graining is desired as the least knock will chip the top paint. Graining will make a much more permanent job".

Top: The Founder, George Humphreys. *Above:* This invoice book dates from the early days when the company painted Admiralty ships. Painting the engine room took 20 men almost 190 hours and cost £4.5.8. *Left:* George Frederick Humphreys *George's eldest son.*

Transport after the war was not cheap and accounts at this time included bus fares to and from the premises being decorated.

The business became a Limited Company in 1948, and later purchased shop premises on Parliament Road

and Waterloo Road. These being run by Fred's wife Elsie and his sister, Vera. The company is presently run by the third generation Stuart, who is Fred and Elsie's son.

Many changes have overtaken traditional methods and materials used in the industry. But decorating will always be a hands on job to achieve the best possible finishes, through time served decorators.

Gone are the days of asking for a shade of paint and waiting for the man to mix it with his stick. Now, with such a wide variety of choice of colours available ready mixed on the shelves, it would seem almost impossible not to be able to find the desired shade.

Modern times
Humphreys have always moved with the times and although it may seem disheartening to watch these changes, it is this way of thinking that has led the company onwards over the years.

There has also been a vein of friendship running through the business. Bill (Curly) Taylor worked for the company for 51 years and his wife Nancy for 47 years until her recent retirement. Which coincided with the firms 75th Anniversary. Other long serving retired staff, who started their apprenticeships and worked for "Humphreys" for so many years are Henry Sykes, Vic Wood and Harry Huggins.

Top: A 1975 letterhead. Nowadays, the namestyle is very similar to this. Above: An estimate for work to be carried out in 1947. Left: Bill (Curly) Taylor - taken on Acklam Road, Middlesbrough. Below: Nancy Taylor, Shop Assistant, pictured around 1960.

Wafers and cones from "over the border"

Liberato Greco was born in Arpino, just south of Rome. This little town was the birthplace of Cicero but Liberato decided that, rather than oratory, he would devote himself to the ice cream industry. Maybe he had too many rivals in Italy, but, for whatever reason, in 1907 he and his brothers, Antonio and Tullio came to the UK. Here he began to sell ices, first from a hand barrow. Soon he graduated to a horse and cart and later still to a motor bicycle and sidecar.

Between the wars

In the early twenties, having learned his trade from a Middlesbrough employer, Liberato decided to set up in business on his own in Suffield Street. After a year or two a change was made from making ice cream to manufacturing wafers and cornets. In all these enterprises Liberato was helped by Antonio and Tullio. Using hand machines, the family found the work hard and the hours long. Over the years a second generation of the family grew up and Liberato's daughter, Hilda, learned her father's trade.

The effects of the Second World War

During the Second World War the male members of the Greco family were interned. The three brothers were travelling aboard the Andorra Star as internees, bound for Canada when the ship was torpedoed by a German U-boat and sank in mid-Atlantic. Five hundred

Top left: Liberato in Model T Ford, Albert park. *Top right:* Pre-cornet days 1926. *Above:* Making cornets the old way. *Right:* Batter mixing in Suffield Street in 1952.
Opposite page top: "Another van loaded!!!" says Tony Rovardi (early 50s). *Opposite page centre:* Liberato Greco with his Grandson Lawrence.
Opposite page bottom: Lawrence and Peter exhibiting at a recent ice cream convention.

miles out from Ireland, the destroyer, the St Lawrence picked up survivors who had been adrift in the sea for over six hours. Sadly one of the brothers, Tullio, was lost. The St Lawrence returned all survivors from the Andorra Star back to Britain. Here, Liberato's daughter Hilda, was capably running the business for

made from its original premises in Suffield Street to the company's present modern factory location in Greta Street. Nowadays, using state of the art cone and wafer ovens the firm manufactures products to sell to many wholesale ice cream manufacturers and retail outlets across the U.K.

The product range these days, is far more extensive than that of the past, whereby the customer can indulge himself in the delights of thick and crispy choc wafers together with a large variety of other products including nougat wafers, oyster delights, sugar cones, twin cones, various sizes of moulded cones, waffles and wafers and other products for the ice cream trade and parlours.

him, and after a few years married a fellow Italian namely Laurence Antonio Rovardi. The couple's sons, Peter and Lawrence currently run the business. Lawrence, incidentally was named after the ship that picked up his grandfather and great uncle during the war.

In 1980 the company was looking towards modernisation and expansion, so a move was

GW Leader - a determination that defied the odds

George William Leader began his working life collecting waste paper on a horse-drawn cart. He was a big man (with a 20 inch neck measurement) and a fit one. At the age of 13 he was second in the British Empire half mile swimming championship. This determination spilled over into his working life. He was a man able to find a living out of almost anything that many people considered waste.

Often, as he went about his business, he would be asked to take away old, wood-framed pictures. He would separate picture and frame and sell them. Then he would get the glass cleaned up and sell that too.

By this means, Mr Leader began gradually to trade in timber and paint. His firm, set up in 1920 was in Commercial Street and soon employed fifty men. Railway lines went directly into the firm where imported timber was unloaded. From there it was sold both to trade and to the general public. The firm made its own paint which everyone in the neighbourhood bought, there being no superstore to provide it.

In the early forties a move was made to Durham Street. During the second world war Mr Leader's three sons were in the army and he had to look after all aspects of the business himself. Whilst Mr Anthony Eden was representing Britain in Geneva at the Committee of Eighteen at the League of Nations to decide on further sanctions against

*Above: The Leader family have always had a strong business presence in the town. This picture shows the grandfather, great grandfather and great grandmother of the founder. **Left:** An advertisement from the early 1940s, promoting such weird and wonderful items as beetle powder and bug oil. **Below:** The firm's Newport Road premises before renovations.*

DO IT YOURSELF !

GLASS (any size cut): 36 x 36, 3/-; 36 x 24, 1/9; 36 x 21, 1/6; 34 x 20, 1/3; 36 x 12, 1/-; 24 x 20, 1/-; 24 x 13, 9d; 20 x 16, 7d; 16 x 14, 5d; 12 x 12, 2½d.
GLASS (24oz.): 40 x 30, 4/-; 24 x 24, 3/6; 42 x 24, 3/-; 36 x 36, 3/-; 24 x 24, 1/2; 24 x 20, 1/-; 24 x 13, 9d; 20 x 16, 7d; 24 x 12, 6d; 20 x 12, 5d; 18 x 14, 5d; 14 x 10, 3d; 12 x 12, 2½d; 12 x 9, 2d. Ask for quantity quotation.
TRELLIS LATHS, 2/6 500 feet.
MOULDINGS and BEADINGS.
PUTTY, 2d lb., 2/- stone.
SASH BARS, 5/6, 7/6. Sash Style 10/-.
SPOUTING, 2d, 3d, 4d and 5d.
ROOFING FELTS, 3/3, 3/9, 5/-.
READY MIXED PAINT, 5d lb., 5/- stone.
PRIMING PAINTS, 3d lb.
NAILS, 2d lb., 2/- stone.
BITUMEN, thick or thin, 1/- gallon.
TAR, 9d gallon, 3/6 five gallons.
LINSEED OIL, 6d pint, 3/- gallon; White Spirit 5d pint. 2/6 gallon; Turps, Sub, 4d pint, 1/6 gallon.
DRYERS, 9d pint, 5/- gallon.
VARNISHES, 11d inside; 1/- outside, 6/- and 6/6 gallon.
PROPERTY VARNISH, 4/6 gallon.
BLACK VARNISHES, 2/- gallon.
CREOSOTE, 10d gallon, 3/9 five-gallon. Light, Medium or Black.
CAUSTIC SODA, ½d lb., 3/- stone.
BEETLE POWDER, 1/- lb.
BUG OIL, 4d pt.; Clear, 1/- pt.
GLASS CLEANING ACID, 1/-.
HINGES, SASHCORDS, CLOTHES-POSTS, CLOTHES-LINES, STRING, TINS, ROPES.
SECTIONAL BUILDINGS, Cycle Sheds, Garages, Poultry Houses, Sports Buildings, Packing Cases, Coal-Bunkers, etc., carefully draughted out. Estimates free. Built, erected, or materials only.
OPEN DAILY UNTIL 8 O'CLOCK.
DELIVERY OR COLLECTION ARRANGED ANYWHERE.
DON'T BE AFRAID TO WRITE TO

LEADER,
COMMERCIAL - STREET, MIDDLESBROUGH
(Opp. Transporter).
MINUTE BUSES (Near DOCKS). TEL. 3174.
31

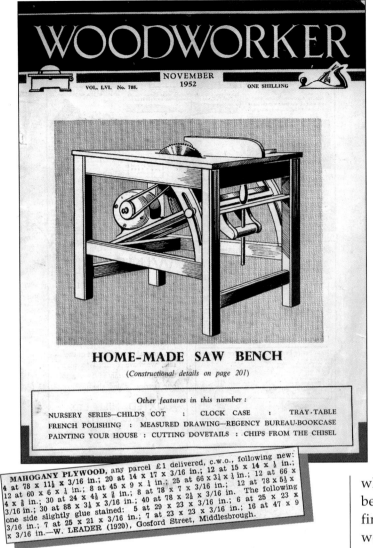

WOODWORKER

VOL. LVI. No. 708.

NOVEMBER 1952

ONE SHILLING

HOME-MADE SAW BENCH
(Constructional details on page 201)

Other features in this number :

NURSERY SERIES—CHILD'S COT : CLOCK CASE : TRAY-TABLE
FRENCH POLISHING : MEASURED DRAWING—REGENCY BUREAU-BOOKCASE
PAINTING YOUR HOUSE : CUTTING DOVETAILS : CHIPS FROM THE CHISEL

MAHOGANY PLYWOOD, any parcel £1 delivered, c.w.o., following new:
4 at 78 x 11½ x 3/16 in.; 20 at 14 x 17 x 3/16 in.; 12 at 15 x 14 x ⅛ in.;
12 at 60 x 6 x ¼ in.; 8 at 45 x 9 x ¼ in.; 25 at 66 x 3¼ x ⅛ in.; 12 at 66 x
4 x ⅜ in.; 30 at 24 x 4½ x ⅜ in.; 8 at 78 x 7 x 3/16 in.; 12 at 78 x 5½ x
3/16 in.; 30 at 88 x 3¼ x 3/16 in.; 40 at 78 x 2¼ x 3/16 in. The following
one side slightly glue stained: 5 at 29 x 23 x 3/16 in.; 6 at 25 x 23 x
3/16 in.; 7 at 25 x 21 x 3/16 in.; 7 at 23 x 23 x 3/16 in.; 16 at 47 x 9
x 3/16 in.—W. LEADER (1920), Gosford Street, Middlesbrough.

Italy, Mr Leader was selling 24 ounce glass at four shillings for a sheet forty inches by thirty, and four inch by seven inch timber at thirty six shillings for 100 ft.

The firm was also selling trellis, moulding and beading, putty at tuppence a pound or two shillings a stone. Ready mixed paint was five shillings a stone. Bitumen (thick or thin) was a shilling a gallon whilst 'bug oil' was fourpence a pint, or a shilling if you wanted it clear.

By now the business had expanded into selling sectional buildings, cycle sheds, garages, poultry houses etc. The last mentioned were in great demand in those times of strict rationing. Mr

Leader was an eccentric who enjoyed nothing more than writing a constant stream of letters to the government to advise them on tank trap manufacture. Though he allowed himself the odd pipe of tobacco, he never drank. He was an opportunist. When Binns had a serious fire, he had bought the fire-damaged stock and held sales 'over the railway', now known as St Hilda's.

When George retired in the early fifties, two of his sons, Harry and Les, took over and ran the business. George had always dealt with the retail side of the business. Harry made paint whilst Les worked in the shop.

When there was a shortage of plywood Harry used to go and get off-cuts of it from F Hills and Son who were major door manufacturers. He would then sell the ply on to Wilkinson Sword, the well known manufacturers of razor blades, to be used in their packaging department.

Since then the business has flourished and expanded with another move to Newport Road where the premises were lavishly refurbished before business began there. David Leader, the first of the third generation of Leaders began to work for the firm in 1965 and so has served it now for 33 years.

Above: A late 1952 brochure for woodworkers with another advertisement from Leader within its pages.
Below: The Newport Road premises.

G.W. LEADER LTD. timber merchants

From a Belgian Black to a Silver Ghost

It was in 1870 that joiner and cabinet maker Joseph Relph set himself up in business as a funeral director. His premises were in Boundary Road, Middlesbrough and in the early days all his coffins were made of solid timber. Nowadays timber is only used for very expensive coffins whilst cheaper ones are made of veneered chipboard.

There have been changes too in the way the coffins are transported. In the 1870s Joseph Relph would go to the bakers' shops in Cannon Street to hire horses for funerals. A Belgian Black horse was a particular favourite.

During the journey a whip had to be kept handy to keep the horses moving. Otherwise they would automatically stop at the bakers' premises expecting their wagons to be loaded with loaves and cakes. A man was employed to 'page' or walk in front of the horse. He had a permanent sheen on the back of his black coat from

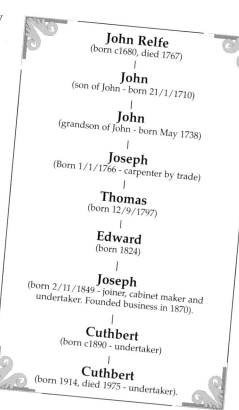

John Relfe
(born c1680, died 1767)
|
John
(son of John - born 21/1/1710)
|
John
(grandson of John - born May 1738)
|
Joseph
(Born 1/1/1766 - carpenter by trade)
|
Thomas
(born 12/9/1797)
|
Edward
(born 1824)
|
Joseph
(born 2/11/1849 - joiner, cabinet maker and undertaker. Founded business in 1870).
|
Cuthbert
(born c1890 - undertaker)
|
Cuthbert
(born 1914, died 1975 - undertaker).

Above: The family tree, showing the generations that have been involved with the business. **Top left:** *Joseph Relph, founder of the company.*
Below: *The Belgian Black horse harnessed to a splendid and dignified carriage.*

stopping and having the horse walk into his back.

The firm has been entrusted with the funeral arrangements for a number of prestigious people, for example Sir Joseph William Isherwood and, in April 1929, Dr Lacey the Bishop of Middlesbrough, and they have buried no less than four Roman Catholic bishops.

For most of this century, of course, coffins and mourners have been driven in dignified black cars. These have included Rolls Royces and a Silver Ghost.

The firm is a member of the National Association of Funeral Directors and the British Institute of embalmers. Its specialities include embalming and repatriation work.

Above: An impressive Rolls Royce used by the firm over the years and inset, two American Buicks.
Top: The funeral of Sir Joseph William Isherwood, directed by Relph's in the 1940s.

Bitten by the betting bug

Reg Boyle became hooked on betting at an early age when he bet threepence each way on Golden Fox who won at odds of 100-7. Reg remembers his very first bet on the racecourse at Thirsk, during World War II, of 2/6 and his first race winner was Kings Jubilee at 8-1.

Christened Owen Boyle Jnr (later nicknamed Reg), son of Owen Boyle an ex professional footballer who played for Bradford Park Avenue, he grew up at 34 Lower Napier Street, South Bank, Middlesbrough on the same street as Wilf Mannion. "I always got a football for Christmas, often borrowed by Wilf and pals to play on the "Puddling" (wasteland)" remembers Reg. After attending St. Peters School, South Bank and St Mary's College, Middlesbrough he commenced work as a messenger boy at Cargo Fleet Steel Works in 1940 and then became an apprentice patternmaker. Reg started to take bets for a Bookmaker on a commission basis and at the age of 17 started up on his own, only to be cleaned out on the fixed odds football coupons so returned to acting as an agent. During World War II Reg couldn't join-up as he was in a "specified trade" but was called up between 1946-1948 where he had the honour of representing the Army at two football matches in

East Africa. After army service and a week at Butlins, Filey, Reg recklessly invested the remainder of his "Demob" money, £110 on two bets and lost the lot with Alf Findlay, that was when he decided that he was much safer taking bets than making them.

Reg recommended taking bets in 1949 whilst working at his trade of patternmaker and in 1952 opened a book on the racecourse with Tommy Dawson (an ex Charlton Athletic footballer who was on the FA Cup winning team in 1947). In September 1952, Reg bet on his own at the Doncaster St. Leger meeting with a set of second hand tools purchased for £6.00 from bookmaker Tom Parkes. From the cheap rings he progressed through to the second rings in the summer and in winter returned to his trade. Unfortunately Reg was again cleaned out on the fixed odds football coupons in September 1953 and had to borrow £5.00 from his sister Madge, for his travel, £1.50 single and lodging, £3.00 per week in advance, to enable him to take up his trade in Birmingham until early 1954.

Still bitten by the betting bug his big break came in 1956 when, following a tip-off from his friend Det. Con. Mick Finn, rented 22 Queen Street, South Bank for £6.00 a week, which belonged to Ron Hislop who had ceased bookmaking. To help pay the rent, Reg sold his Austin Somerset car. On his first day Reg had only two customers, Alice Ford and Mrs Outhwaite who between them bet the princely sum of one pound and twelve shillings.

In 1957 Reg married local girl Irene Escritt and they now have four children, daughters Susan, Angela and Lynne who all joined the business

> ## "THE LOCAL POLICE SERGEANT, TED COCKERILL WANDERED IN, DRESSED IN FULL UNIFORM, THE PLACE EMPTIED IN SECONDS..."

from school, and son Simon who joined after University. Susan, their eldest daughter became manageress at 19 years of age.

The company became incorporated on the 17th May 1960. Until the Betting Act came into force in 1961, betting was illegal but police allowed it to go on in certain areas provided it was conducted in an orderly manner (and kept illegal gambling off the streets). On one occasion Reg remembers one Saturday afternoon when he and a clerk had a packed shop the local police sergeant, Ted Cockerill wandered in in full uniform, "the place emptied in seconds" recalled Reg " and all Ted

*Opposite top: Reg Boyle at Epsom Derby in the mid 1950s. **Opposite bottom:** Reg Boyle collecting the Carlisle Bell in 1971. **Below:** Reneé presenting Champagne to the winning trainer of The Reg Boyle Trophy, E Weymes, at Redcar in 1981.*

wanted to do was place a half crown bet. I said to him 'don't ever do that again Ted, if you want to make a bet can you please do it by telephone!'".

After the Betting Act of 1961, Reg and John Mallon were prosecuted for allowing a person under the age of 18 on licensed premises. The person was asked if he was 18 and replied that he was, he then placed a bet when the Police walked in. At court they were found not guilty. This case was the first of its kind and is on record as the 'Crown versus Boyle and Mallon'.

In 1961 Reg Boyle was able to obtain licenses for 5 shops in South Bank, Dormantstown and Saltburn. Today Reg Boyle Ltd. operate 23 shops in an area ranging from West Cornforth, County Durham to Loftus in East Cleveland and has twenty Tattersalls pitches at racecourses from Ayr

> **"REG MAINTAINS THAT HE WAS LUCKY TO SURVIVE THE EARLY DAYS OF HIS BUSINESS, DUE TO LACK OF SECURITY"**

to Cheltenham. In this Reg has been assisted by his son Simon and his clerk for the past 21 years Jack Bolton, a well known ex amateur footballer.

Reg's interest in horse racing has extended from betting to sponsoring races at Teesside Park, Redcar and Sedgefield and by owning a number of successful horses, winning more than twenty races. His first horse, Kilindini won as a two year old at Ayr on her second outing in 1962. Reg bought her for 220 Guineas and she went on to win four more races with prize money totalling more than £2,000, and was later sold for 1,800 Guineas.

In 1971, in partnership with a friend Derek Hawkey he won the Carlisle Bell, the oldest race in Great Britain with El Credo. Lester Piggott rode one of Reg's horses, Sir Blast, to the winners enclosure in 1967, at Beverley.

Owen Boyle Jnr (Reg) was chairman of the now defunct Teesside and District Bookmakers Association and is at present a director of Northern BPA. From 1965 - 1972 Reg was a Director of the South Bank Sporting Club, booking such famous acts as Tony Christie and the Penmen in 1969, for £125 per week and for £120 Engelbert Humperdink before he broke into the charts with "Please Release Me".

Reg has always been a keen sportsman, playing local amateur football and at 52 years of age he took up running, winning races in his age group over distances ranging from 10k, 10 miles, half marathon, mini marathon (17½ miles), 20 miles and marathon. Reg has raised many thousands of pounds for local and national charities through sponsorship and in 1986 was a nominee for Cleveland Sportsman of the Year, he is still jogging today.

The company has grown steadily since 1956 when turnover was £18,672.1.5 and despite competition from the big firms who have a very strong foothold and make expansion difficult, the company is still looking for suitable sites for expansion and are negotiating the acquisition of four more shops in 1998.

Reg maintains that he was lucky to survive the early days of his business, due to lack of security, there was no high-tech video and camera surveillance in those days and owes the company's success to his faithful early staff, Phonsie, Hughie and John Mallon, and the fact that he built up a connection of fifteen agents with clock bags in the local docks and steelworks plus the constant support from his wife Reneé during the past 40 years, who is also the company secretary.

Opposite page Reneé presenting The Reg Boyle Bookmaker Chase to the owner of Queen's Bay Lady at Sedgefield in 1990. **Below:** Reg and Reneé with their extended family including nine grandchildren at the splendid Rushpool Hall, Saltburn, owned by a friend Jim Brennan on the occasion of their Ruby Wedding Anniversary. This was a surprise party organised by their children and followed a Celebration Mass by Fr Ricardo Morgan at St. Andrews, Teesville.

From wartime parachutes to a nineties research nerve-centre

ICI's origins on the south bank of the River Tees stemmed from the massive upsurge in the use of man-made plastics during the Second World War. Many products made from oil were being developed, including 'Perspex' for cockpit covers in aircraft, polyethylene which made airborne radar possible and man-made fibres such as nylon for parachutes and uniforms. During the war, these were being produced in small factories all over the country so that if a bomb hit one all would not be lost.

As early as 1943, however, the Main Board of ICI was looking for a site for production to be centralised when these new materials would be required in large quantities in peacetime. A 'green field' site of 2,000 acres on the south bank of the Tees was chosen, six miles south-east of Billingham. In its favour were good port facilities on the river, rail access, a developing system of roads to connect with the new motorways

and a Canadian Air Force station soon to be converted to a civil airport. The site was flat and on boulder clay, ideal as a foundation for heavy structures. Water and coal were available and local people had the required skills.

To obtain the land ICI had to purchase a further 2,000 acres. The company did not want that part in the hills which was honeycombed with old iron mines and subject to subsidence. This area is farmed with sheep and pigs on the steep hillsides where the plough cannot work. This is some recom-

Above right: Wilton Castle, part of Colonel Lowther's entire Teesside estate, purchased by ICI in order to develop the Wilton Site.
Below: The frontage of the Wilton Centre overlooking the lake which is a haven for wildlife.

pense for the farmland that was used for the building of the company's factory.

Work began on the Wilton site in February 1946 and by September 1947 the Apprentice Training School was completed. The School was superseded by the new larger Wilton Training Centre, now Teesside Training and Enterprise, an independently run organisation which gives hundreds of young people each year the skills required by a large modern chemical complex.

In July 1949 the Phenol Formaldehyde Plant began to operate and in August the 'Perspex' plant came on line. There has been a regular progression since of opening new plants and closing outmoded ones.

The essential purpose of Wilton is to make from oil any materials that customers require. The oil comes from the North Sea but the company buys products taken from oil from various different countries. The presence of oil in the North Sea was not known when the Wilton site was chosen but it was well placed when the discovery was made.

At Seal Sands, ICI and Phillips Petroleum have a five million tons a year refinery using oil from the Norwegian sector. ICI takes the light oil, called naphtha, using it in the aromatics and olefine plants. It supplies the raw material for plastics such as polyethylene and polypropylene, man-made fibres such as nylon, detergents, paint, petrol and very many other intermediate products. These are delivered to customers who treat them still further before they get to the high street shops.

The main service facilities consist of the site power station. Half the fuel for the station is waste oil and gas. The boiler section acts as a large incinerator as well as a producer of steam and electricity. It helps the company to dispose of waste materials from oil and gas that can't be made into anything saleable.

The company has on-site amenities for staff, medical and personnel services and even a fire brigade. Wilton is also the nerve centre of a large scale research and technology effort which makes a vital contribution to the activities of ICI's growing international businesses.

Top: Building the 'Perspex' building in 1947 - one of the first major construction projects on the site.
Above: The Olefines 6 ethylene cracker at night.
Left: An aerial view of the Wilton site.

Atha & Co - the family firm with traditional values

Atha and Co., was founded by Tony Atha who in 1958, qualified as a Solicitor having served five years as an Articled Pupil with Messrs. Sykes Johnston and Lee Solicitors of York. After serving two years National Service as an Officer in the Army Tony Atha was admitted as a Solicitor of the Supreme Court of Judicature in 1960. He was fortunate to be offered the opportunity by his old firm to set up a new office in Redcar as a partner with his former principals in the practice of Sykes Lee and Atha whose main responsibility was to service the conveyancing requirements of a large building firm called Bradley Builders (York) Limited.

In a small first floor office suite in Redcar with the assistance one secretary and over a period of three years Tony Atha conveyed over 300 properties on the Ings Farm Estate and during that period acquired a good number of private clients. When the estate was completed as per the arrangement with his former partners they vacated the partnership and left him as sole principal in the practice which was renamed Atha and Co.

Tony Atha's builder client was delighted with the work carried out on its behalf and when it moved on to open sites in Scarborough, York, Marske-by-the-Sea and Stockton-on-Tees it invited Tony Atha to carry out the legal work in the development of these estates on the basis that he would open a local office to deal with each estate.

Assistant Solicitors were recruited and ultimately Tony Atha became the common partner in a number of individual partnerships established in Redcar, Marske by the Sea, Skelton in Cleveland, Middlesbrough, Scarborough, Guisborough and York. The established practices of Cress Tarn Stockton, Eagle Clark and Co., Filey and Clifford Smith in Burnley Lancashire were subsequently acquired to complete a network of 12 offices all serving local building sites developed by Bradley

Tony Atha
Founded the business in the early 1960s
|
Charles Atha
joined his father in the early 1980s
|
Tony Atha "retired" in the mid 1980s
|
Jane Atha
joined her brother, Charles in 1996

and Co. (Builders) York. Regrettably the building firm got into financial difficulties in the late 1970s and was no longer a source of business but fortunately the individual practices and their local partners had become sufficiently established to survive without their main source of business.

In the early 1980s Tony Atha's son Charles took his Degree in Law and decided to serve his Articles with the Newcastle firm of Ward Hadway. Whilst Tony Atha was disappointed at the time that his son chose to serve his Articles with another firm, it proved to be the right decision since it gave him an insight into fields of legal work not practised by his father's firm.

On qualifying and being admitted as a Solicitor, his son Charles decided to come back to join his father who gave him the Middlesbrough office which was then staffed by an Assistant Solicitor, two fee earners, three secretaries, a receptionist and a book keeper.

In-the mid 1980s Tony Atha decided to retire from his individual partnerships and sold out his interest to his then partners some of whom retained the name in the firm i.e. Atha Strong and Co., at Marske, Atha Summers and Co., at Scarborough, Atha Barton and Co., at Guisborough and Evans Atha and Co., at York.

"WITH THE HELP OF ONE SECRETARY, TONY ATHA CONVEYED OVER 300 PROPERTIES IN A THREE YEAR PERIOD."

Tony Atha continued to look after clients who were personal friends from his office adjoining his home in Saltburn whilst also assisting his son in the conveyancing side of the business at Middlesbrough.

Charles on the other hand developed an interest in personal injury work and industrial disease claims and the Middlesbrough practice expanded rapidly to service this work. It currently employs five qualified solicitors, four experienced fee earners, and a supporting staff of around 30 with a turnover exceeding one million pounds per annum.

Atha & Co., Solicitors which is now wholly owned by Charles Atha, for tax reasons became one of the first firms in England to convert to a Corporate body recognised by the Law Society.

Charles's sister, Jane, at the age of 30 decided to give up her career in travel, married in 1996 settled in Wilmslow in Cheshire and decided to take up a new career as a Licenced Conveyancer. Whilst chasing the academic qualification it became necessary to gain some practical experience and since she could not get a job, Charles and his father decided to acquire a small conveyancing and probate practice in Wilmslow.

Jane now runs the practice assisted by the former owner Arthur Mellor and her father who visits the office two days a week. Charles occasionally flies his own light aircraft across to Woodford which is about 5 miles from the Wilmslow office.

It is hoped that father might eventually be able to retire (again) from both the Middlesbrough office and the Wilmslow office leaving his son and daughter to perpetuate the name of Atha and Co., into a third generation.

Above: Tony Atha (centre) with Charles and Jane (front) with some of the staff of Atha & Co. (Wilmslow).
Facing page: The premises in Middlesbrough.

More than a century of success in the construction industry

In 1890, (backed by a small loan from his father) 20 year old Austin Graham set about his business of installing dynamos to provide electric lighting and electricity supplies to the great country houses and business premises of the Teesside area.

This was in the days when the majority of Middlesbrough's streets and buildings were illuminated by gas lamps and the town centre docks were crammed with sailing ships from around the British Empire. Austin Graham's pioneering business prospered but was hit by his untimely death in 1918, when he was killed in action while serving as a Lieutenant Colonel in the Green Howards.

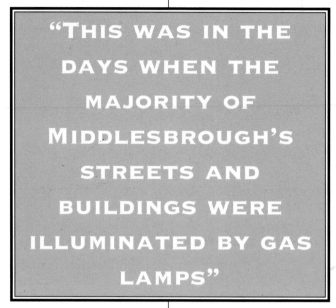

"THIS WAS IN THE DAYS WHEN THE MAJORITY OF MIDDLESBROUGH'S STREETS AND BUILDINGS WERE ILLUMINATED BY GAS LAMPS"

work until Grahams ceased their involvement in such work during the 1960s when it was taken over by the Area Electricity Boards. It is with some irony that Graham Brothers became a fully owned subsidiary of the Eve Group PLC in 1992, as Eve Transmission is one of the three major exponents of overhead transmission line systems. The name was changed to Eve Graham to reflect this merger.

Today the company involves itself in total design and build projects including providing mechanical and electrical packages for national building and construction companies. They have also worked for major firms based adjacent to one of Britains largest and busiest

His brothers, Thomas and Peter, had joined him before the outbreak of hostilities and they took over the running of the business. Since those days three more generations of Grahams have been involved in the business until the link with the Graham family was broken in 1986, when Harry and Charles Graham sold the business. Until this time Graham's "little blue vans" were a familiar site in and around the town of Middlesbrough.

Around 50 years ago Graham Brothers and the Eve Group were in direct competition with each other on the very important high-voltage

ports on the estuary of the Tees, like ICI, Tees Storage and British Steel, plus the massive Nissan Plant at Sunderland. Eve Graham have also done the refurbishment of listed buildings in the centre of Middlesbrough itself.

Another coup for Eve Graham and an important landmark to the people of Middlesbrough has been the building of the Cellnet Riverside Stadium for Middlesbrough FC, where Eve Graham have provided the mechanical and electrical engineering and plumbing for the prestigious project.

Staff at Eve Graham take great pride in the long history of their company and derive satisfaction in telling clients that Grahams have been trading continuously for over a hundred years.

The company is determined to sustain the steady growth of the last few years and are set to expand the maintenance division so they can provide a full mechanical, electrical engineering and plumbing service with 24-hour emergency cover. They have also recently taken on water industry projects worth £6 million and hope that this diversification will play a significant part in their development. By having such a wide range of services in a very competitive market and with highly trained and motivated staff Eve Graham feel confident that they have all the key elements that will help them progress further in the future.

Opposite page: Eve Graham's head office.
Above: The refurbished Chamber of Commerce building.
Left: Amos Hinton's old store which is now the Midland Bank.

ACKNOWLEDGMENTS

The publishers would like to thank the following people
for their help in making this book possible:

Ranald Allen - Editor, The Evening Gazette, Teesside;

Richard Pears - Senior Assistant Librarian, Middlesbrough Reference Library;

Jane Whitfield - Librarian, The Northern Echo.